Miracles Among Us

✦

A Look Inside the Lebanon Soup Kitchen

Nancey West

iUniverse, Inc.
New York   Bloomington

Miracles Among Us
A Look Inside the Lebanon Soup Kitchen

iUniverse books may be ordered through booksellers or by contacting:

iUniverse
1663 Liberty Drive
Bloomington, IN 47403
www.iuniverse.com
1-800-Authors (1-800-288-4677)

ISBN: 978-0-595-52226-2 (pbk)
ISBN: 978-0-595-62284-9 (ebk)

Printed in the United States of America
iUniverse rev. date 10/30/08

Contents

Acknowledgement

I would like to thank my three dearest friends:
Christine M. Carpenter
Grace Johnson
Jane LaMunyon

They have inspired and encouraged me in the writing of this book. They have given me strength and confidence through their prayers and wisdom. May God bless them for their patience and their faith.

Also, I would like to thank the many people who took the time to share their lives with me. I have been touched and changed by their poignant stories.

Introduction

Lord,
Make me an instrument of your peace.
Where there is hatred, let me sow love;
Where there is injury, pardon;
Where there is doubt, faith;
Where there is despair, hope;
Where there is darkness, light;
Where there is sadness, joy;
O Divine master, grant that I may not so much seek to be
consoled as to console,
To be understood, as to understand,
To be loved, as to love;
For it is in giving that we receive, it is in pardoning that we
are pardoned,
And it is in dying that we are born to eternal life.

St. Francis of Assisi

Strangers come together for a meal three days a week at the Lebanon Soup Kitchen. Some eat and leave with few words spoken. Some share greetings. Others share stories. All share the inherent need for a meal. That is what unites them in a unique bond.

Each person understands and does not condemn the other for their mistakes, bad choices or hardships. These are not merely the homeless, the down-and-out or the bums. These are people. People who feel, who love and who need help.

Some accept assistance and take action to improve their lives. Some are happy with their hand-out lifestyle and grateful to get a warm meal. Others need to make their income last longer by supplementing meals between monthly checks.

The bond formed by similar circumstances brings some back for the fellowship with their Soup Kitchen friends, even after their need for the assistance is gone.

The compassionate volunteers who come to prepare, cook, serve, or cleanup can't ignore the sadness and heart-wrenching stories they hear. They also see a ready smile, the sparkling eyes filled with appreciation or hear a hearty laugh following some joke or story.

Trust must be built to heal a soul left open and raw, as it can be in people with deep needs. They must have a safe place to come, eat, get warm in the cold winter months and shed their daily problems, if only for a short time. Many have found comfort in the Soup Kitchen and in the people, both those who come and who serve. Time wise, their visit at the Soup Kitchen may only be a blip in their lives but it can make a life-long difference.

The dining hall rings with the many voices enjoying meals in a safe atmosphere. The people who fill the hall are as different as any other segment of society. There are those who do the best they can to improve their lives and there are others satisfied with theirs. Some find themselves in trouble with the law due to their situation or their choices. Inside, the building remains a safe haven from the police, who must wait outside to question or arrest anyone.

This atmosphere of great human need and greater compassion is an area where God moves, working among those who are seeking help. God's love is not preached in fancy words but shown in caring actions. Miracles can be seen often, when the eyes and heart are open to feel God's presence.

This book is to show that 'those people' are God's precious children. They may be discarded by society, never by God.

'For I was hungry and you gave me nothing to eat, I was thirsty and you gave me nothing to drink, I was a stranger and you did not invite me in, I needed clothes and you did not clothe me, I was sick and in prison and you did not look after me.'

They also will answer, 'Lord, when did we see you hungry or thirsty or a stranger or needing clothes or sick or in prison and did not help you?'

He will reply, 'I tell you the truth, whatever you did not do for one of the least of these, you did not do for me.' Matthew 25:42-45 (NIV)

Preface

My business is not to remake myself,
But make the absolute best of what God made.

Robert Browning

Marcy hung up the phone near the dining room door at the Soup Kitchen, "This lady said we can have all the cherries off her tree if we pick them." She shrugged her shoulders. "We can't ask volunteers to climb a tree."

"Where is it?" I asked, already forming a plan.

"Behind the Mexican restaurant on Santiam. It's the only house along there."

"I'll go take a look at it and see what I can do." I called to my kids playing in the foyer, "Kristi, Matt let's go."

I stopped in front of a small garage built during a time when garages were made to hold a car and little more. Next to it, a narrow lawn wrapped around the front and side of a tiny, white house. A single tree, with its canopy covering the yard, stood beside the house. The limbs sagged with the weight of the bright red cherries. *There are a lot of them,* I marveled as I studied the trunk and main branches. *It would be easy to climb. And with an orchard ladder, we should be able to pick buckets full.*

"May I help you?" A gentle voice drew my attention to the doorway of the house. An elderly lady peered through the screen.

"I'm from the Soup Kitchen. Someone called about donating cherries."

A younger woman stepped past the lady. "It's okay Mom, I called them about using the cherries. My name is Delores." She held out a thin, tanned hand.

I shook her hand and introduced myself.

"Can you get them picked in the next couple of days?"

"I'll be here tomorrow afternoon," I assured her.

Now to get the crew! I began calling our high school youth group and soon had several willing helpers.

We arrived on schedule with ladders and buckets. Crimson streaks began staining our hands and clothes and soon the juicy, red fruit filled all our containers. We took our harvest to the Soup Kitchen for volunteers to use in delicious entrees.

The cherries were only part of the donations given the Soup Kitchen by a supportive community. Fresh fruits and vegetables were brought and used right away. Non-perishables were stored in one of the converted closets at the front of the church. Frozen foods quickly filled the one freezer. More freezer space was needed, but the fledgling operation could not afford industrial freezers.

A few volunteers offered the use of freezers in their homes. "We need to keep a list of what is in each freezer so we know where to go. We'll start with the closest ones." Marcy added firmly, "This list has to be kept accurate."

Most of the time, this inconvenient system worked well.

One afternoon I was called about a donation of frozen foods. "Could someone meet me at the church in half an hour?" The lady asked. "No problem," I responded. I was busy on the farm and Marcy was out of town so I tried calling different volunteers who were familiar with the system. No one was available. In desperation, I called Dirk. I repeated the arrangements and he assured me he would pick up and deliver the food to the designated house for storage.

I returned to my work and forgot about the food. An hour later, I received a call from the homeowner where the freezer was located. "When did you say he would be here with the food?"

"He should have been there ten minutes after I talked to you."

"He hasn't shown up."

Maybe he went to the wrong house. Frantically, I called other freezer owners on the list. No one had seen him. The summer day was hot and sunny. *Those frozen items couldn't be frozen anymore. What could have happened to him? Was he in an accident?*

I called everyone I could think of and no one knew where Dirk or the food was.

Eventually, Dirk called me, sounding perfectly healthy.

"Where's the food?" I asked.

"I gave it away," he dryly replied, as if that had been a stupid question.

"What do you mean? You were to take it to the freezer."

"I saw some people in front of a house. I stopped and asked if they wanted some of it. Then others came by and I gave it all away." His voice oozed with pride of his thoughtful charity.

Silence echoed through the phone. Guilt began to seep in around the initial surprise. *Why didn't I do it myself?* I thanked Dirk for the effort and tried consoling myself. *At least the food didn't go to waste.*

At the next board meeting, we decided that only designated people could transport food from the Soup Kitchen to the freezers or back.

This situation, like others, had a solution. Finding solutions established better ways of doing business. Doing business began to flow smoothly. Recording donations, scheduling cooks and volunteers and meeting all the government regulations were a routine part of operations. The Soup Kitchen established its foundation.

"Nancey, your kid is out front again." I heard the now familiar warning that one, and it was always easy to guess which one, of my children had wandered outside with the guests waiting in line.

I hurried out to get my four-year-old son, Matt. His blond head was tilted back as he stared up at a tall, thin man leaning against the brick building. "You shouldn't smoke. It's bad for you," I heard him say as I reached for his small arm to lead him back inside. The man took a long drag on his cigarette, his expression unchanged as he looked down at the bold child.

"Yea, you better listen to the kid," someone laughed as Matt and I returned to the building.

The Soup Kitchen was operating smoothly but my struggle each night to keep Matt and his six-year-old sister, Kristi, entertained was getting harder. For a while they contently played in the nursery upstairs or looked at books. Matt brought trucks to play with on the floor. When I could arrange it, they went to friends' houses to play. But the amount of time I spent at the Soup Kitchen began to wear on the kids and me.

They didn't mind the activities with the church youth group when we picked cherries. But riding in the car while I picked up donated food from businesses or spending hours at the church grew boring for them. Keeping an eye on the kids distracted me from my work in the kitchen.

I also spent time training as a volunteer for the Referral Center that was scheduled to open in the church. Between the training and the kids I did not feel I had the time to be an adequate leader for the Soup Kitchen or an attentive mother. It was time for me to resign and let someone take over who could be more focused.

"We are sorry to see you leave, but accept your resignation," Marcy said as she handed me a farewell card signed by many of the volunteers. She continued with the November board meeting.

Those words made it final; I was out. I had not anticipated the void I felt. What I thought would be a needed relief was instead sadness. I would miss the busy role I played.

Though I no longer had an active part, I remained interested in the work God was doing through the people there. I remained friends with several of the volunteers and listened to their stories of both sadness and joy.

When my children where grown, I returned to college, studying journalism. God had given me the ability and desire to write and I finally pursued the possibilities. I wrote briefly for a newspaper and some magazines. When I attended the dedication ceremony for the Soup Kitchen addition, I saw God's vision for me.

God had worked in many hearts to start the Soup Kitchen and had worked in many more through the years. It was truly God's Soup Kitchen and His part in the story needed to be told. I had never written a book before but I knew in Psalms 32:8 the Lord promised, "I will instruct you and teach you in the way you should go; I will counsel you and watch over you."

I began interviewing volunteers who served through the years. The love of giving to others was a common thread in their many stories. I knew there were more heart-felt stories among the people who came to eat. I volunteered to serve but I was reluctant to visit with the guests.

When one of the guests died, his funeral was held at the church. I was there for other reasons but was impressed with the number of people who attended. Many told stories of a kind, caring man. The attachment to their friend and the sadness from their loss could be felt in their loving words.

Later, at the Soup Kitchen, I looked for the different ones who spoke at the funeral. The opportunity to talk about their friend allowed many to open up to me. I learned about many situations as I tried to piece the deceased's life together.

I listened and recorded what people were willing to tell me. I could not verify many of the testimonies, nor did I try to dispute them. I wrote what I was told. Some names have been changed, some were never known. Details may have been added but the human essence of the stories remain true, as I understood or experienced them.

Whatever else I may have learned from these stories, the greatest lesson is, "except for the grace of God, there go I."

A volunteer once told me, "Everyone should go and eat there to see how close we are to being them."

This is not only the Soup Kitchen story, it is my story. Perhaps you'll find yourself in these stories, also.

In His service,
Nancey West

Dedicated to all the wonderful people who have touched my life and many other lives through the miracles at God's Soup Kitchen.

Miracles Among Us

Out on the streets, there was a need,
In willing hearts, God planted a seed.
Working together to make it come true,
Volunteers gathered to start something new.

They collected bread, vegetables and meat,
Not knowing how many would come to eat.
Each meal was cooked to be the best,
And they trusted God to do the rest.

He brought people together in His grace,
Loving and comforting any age, sex or race.
The lonely, disabled, abused and abandoned,
Came together, knowing each one was welcomed.

One man once had a wife and a son,
But lost them both by a hit and run.
He buried his heart in the grave with them,
And buried his life in a cheap bottle of gin.

Another gave his wife a nice home and cars,
But a work accident left his brain with scars.
He could no longer work and needed some care.
She took everything and treated him unfair.

Both men are alone and living on the street,
Waiting in this line for a warm meal to eat.
Their lives are shattered with pain and despair,
Searching for a purpose and someone to care.

A young girl holds a baby while pushing another.
Her soft face looks too young to be a mother.
The father left, said they were a burden.
With little education, her future is uncertain.

A slender man comes, it's all he's ever known,
Taking advantage of the kindness he is shown.
He learned the system from his mother,
Never changing his lifestyle for any other.

Pre-teen children timidly creep in alone,
No one is around to cook their meal at home.
With a house that is empty and often no heat,
They come to get warm as well as to eat.

 Here, elderly couples and young families
Come to save money to buy necessities.
It might be shoes or a winter coat,
Pencils, paper or a school tote.

The Soup Kitchen clothed one for a job interview,
Gave a reference, a tip and a "God Bless You."
She was hired and for five years has worked there,
An asset giving to community and her family's welfare.

Nothing is asked of those passing through the door,
Just "what can we do for you?" and nothing more.
Their problems and despairs can be left outside,
No one is concerned with what they have to hide.

Neighbors and community have given so much,
Hundreds of people have felt the touch.
Volunteers give from whatever their means,
From the one who donates to the one who cleans.

And One gently moving through the room,
Has come to comfort those in their doom.
Love, care and compassion, He brings to this place,
By a friendly greeting or a smile on a face.

When something is needed, there's no reason to fret.
Whether physical or spiritual, each need will be met.
For the Designer has been there from the very start,
But He can not be seen with eyes, only the heart.

He brings someone to comfort with a kind thought,
And give others a light of hope so desperately sought.
He works softly and quietly, doesn't make a fuss,
Yet, we can see Him through the miracles among us.

Sees the Hungry

God's hand can be seen moving among the needy
where desperation has made them open to receive.

Author Unknown

The empty swings swayed gently in the breeze as the winter chill
crept through River Park. The sand pit, climbing bars and fort sat
silent following a summer of energetic and noisy children exploring their
every corner. The lone boat dock floated in the swift waters, too cold
now for most recreationalists. Warm weather opportunities for fun and
relaxation were stilled by the falling temperatures and people seeking
the warmth of their homes. The manicured grass flowed among the
picnic tables, through the baseball field and along trails that gave way
to dense hazel brush and alder trees where opportunities of another kind
could be found.

Tucked away from sight in the overgrowth, the homeless sought sanctuary
in primitive camps and make-do shelters of brush and cardboard. The
shrubbery became a welcomed barrier from the wind but held little comfort
in the rain, snow or freezing temperatures to those unable to find warmth
anywhere else. The park is located at the east end of Grant Street, where
the only bridge into Lebanon spans the Santiam River. A few people found
refuge under the bridge. Others found shelter around the edge of Lebanon to
form transient communities. The number of people in these camps were only
estimated and seldom talked about.

Hidden from sight, the community often thought these people did
not exist. In Lebanon, where a sign at the edge of town read "the city that

1

friendliness built," were they just homeless people in a heartless community? Or did the community just need to open their eyes to the need?

One person became their advocate for having a healthy meal. Marcy Huntsinger was not a stranger to the streets. She moved to Lebanon from California and spoke little of her past, except that she "knew first hand what it was like to be without."

She volunteered at the St. Mary's Soup Kitchen in Albany and the Stone Soup Kitchen in Corvallis. Both provided ways for her to return to others what had been given to her. She cooked, served meals and worked wherever needed each week. But that wasn't enough.

Marcy's house in Lebanon provided her with an awareness of people in need. She lived along Grant Street, several blocks from the river. Marcy watched from her porch the many people making the nightly trek from their secluded make-shift homes to the center of the community. Some she recognized from St. Mary's. But few people from Lebanon were able to travel the 15 miles to Albany for a free warm meal. The trip placed strains on their meager finances. Besides the gas it cost, it added to the wear and tear on their cars, usually already beyond reliable use. Others had no access to transportation to Albany, leaving them to scrounge for whatever they could find in Lebanon.

Unable to sleep one night, Marcy bundled in her heavy coat and followed a group along the street. The procession led to two grocery stores that sat across from each other on the corner of Main and Oak Streets. Both Safeway and Stiffler's had dumpsters behind them for discarding outdated food and other garbage. These containers of refuse provided a source for meals, mostly meat, to those without access to healthy options. Marcy watched in the shadows as they wiped garbage and waste from packages before placing them in sacks to carry back to their primitive homes. Sorrow and determination welled in her as tears spilled onto her cheeks. She vowed to do everything she could to provide a meal in Lebanon for those desperate enough to eat discarded and possibly spoiled food.

Marcy returned to St. Mary's Soup Kitchen and told others what she had seen and her dream of a soup kitchen in Lebanon. Doris Hull, manager of St. Mary's, said that she would help in any way. Helen Richards, a deacon from St. Edward's Episcopal Church in Lebanon also worked at St. Mary's. She agreed with Marcy's plans and joined her in the quest to establish a way for people to obtain healthy meals in Lebanon.

Years earlier, when Helen began studying to become a deacon for the Episcopal Church, she needed a 'mission' to work with. She chose the soup kitchen in Albany. Her heart ached for the people and she was thankful for the small difference she could make in their lives. The work and the people grew to mean so much to her that when her mission was over, she continued to serve. She had been there five years when she met Marcy.

Marcy and Helen began to search Lebanon for a church to host a soup kitchen. The churches they were familiar with did not have a serving area and kitchen large enough to feed the numbers of people expected. That led Marcy to write a letter to the editor of the local paper.

Part of the letter read, "Is there one church in Lebanon with heart and kitchen enough to serve an estimated 40-50 people?"

Then they waited weeks. No answer came.

XXXXXX

About this time, the high school group at the First Christian Church was talking about ideas of what it could do for the community. The youth group agreed that it would be nice to serve a free soup and sandwich lunch some Saturday. They could not agree on a weekend so decided to wait until fall to organize one meal.

That discussion deeply touched me. Having one meal is like teasing people who really needed balanced nutrition regularly. The idea suddenly seemed urgent to me that Lebanon needed a regular soup kitchen, run by committed adults.

Mildred West, my mother-in-law, gave a copy of the local newspaper with Marcy's letter to my husband, Jon, who was the chairman of the board at the First Christian Church. Jon worried that the congregation would not be receptive to the idea but with encouragement from his mother and me. Jon presented the letter to the church board, suggesting they consider it.

Resistance came in the form of many questions. Some were 'what ifs'. "What if those people came in the sanctuary and tracked mud?" "What if those people snuck around the church and stole something?" "What if people who didn't need help came?" But the scriptures reminded the congregation that "those people" were the ones James was talking about in James 2:15-16. "What good is it, my brothers, if a man claims to have faith but has not deeds? Can such faith save him? Suppose a brother or sister is without clothes and daily food. If one of you says to him, 'Go, I wish you well; keep warm and well fed,' but does nothing about his physical needs, what good is it?"

Paul questioned faith's sincerity without following it with action. How could we turn someone away because of 'what ifs' that we did not know would ever happen? Jesus gave the example of welcoming Judas to His table when He knew that Judas would betray him.

Jon had no answer for other questions concerning regulations, number of volunteers needed and where the food would come from. He asked Marcy to speak to the members about the details. She stood strong in her determination to feed the homeless when she addressed the congregation. Her deep voice flowed with conviction as she squared her shoulders to lobby for a soup kitchen in Lebanon. Marcy never took 'no' for an answer. Every obstacle had a possible solution.

Finally, the church agreed they could not run a proper soup kitchen with just their congregation. A public meeting was planned to find the amount of community support.

People squeezed near one another to find a place to stand in the small room where the public meeting was held. Seven members of the First Christian Church were in attendance; some to offer their help, others to protect the church's interests. People came from St. Martin's Episcopal, Our Savior's Lutheran, Assembly of God and St. Edward's Catholic Churches and from the community. A group from St. Mary's Soup Kitchen was there to offer support.

The overflow of enthusiasm terminated any argument of whether or not to go forward with plans to coordinate a soup kitchen. The only questions were when and how.

The First Christian Church's dining area would seat over 100, the kitchen had utensils and equipment to prepare large meals. Electrical phases in the kitchen needed to be upgraded. Some of those present insisted that the repairs, permits, licenses and anything else that was needed be in place before an opening date set.

I had no intention of talking that night, but the idea of not setting a date to open stirred something within me. Postponing the opening could drag on for a long time. I suddenly blurted out, 'It is God's kitchen; let Him work out the details.' Instantly, I became deeply involved.

Someone else quickly added, "If it's not ready, we will serve sandwiches from the back of a pickup!"

Before a date was chosen, a board needed to be established. The chair of that board would be someone from the First Christian Church's congregation. Looking at those people in attendance, the possibilities were limited. I sat quietly, my anxiety building. Inside I was arguing with God that I was not the one to lead. He knew I wasn't qualified, yet I knew He worked through anyone. Rather than see progress stop in order to find a chairman, I agreed to take the job.

The board established that night was: Nancey West, chair, Helen Richards, Pastor Doug Dornhecker and Marcy Huntsinger.

An opening date was set for Wednesday, June 7, 1989, to coincide with the annual Strawberry Festival. The volunteers who signed up that night, agreed to start work immediately. Dorothy Hull, who helped establish St. Mary's Soup Kitchen, helped with the legalities of establishing a non-profit organization and gave advice on how to make it run smoothly.

People filed out of the room, excitedly talking about where God's hand may be leading them.

Sample Menu:
Hawaiian Chicken
Rice
Mixed Vegetables
Green Salad
Fruit
Dessert

Finds a Recipe

The Miracle is not that we do this work, but that we are happy to do it.

Mother Teresa

As I drove to the first meeting of the newly formed Lebanon Soup Kitchen board, my heart beat with excitement at the reality of a soup kitchen taking shape. With a smile, I pictured the compassionate volunteers, the nutritious meals and the thankful recipients.

My drive took me past the park where some of the homeless camps were situated. I scanned the wooded area along both sides of the river. No sign of dwellings or life were visible. *How many are out there? What if there are more than we think? Will we be able to serve them? Where are we going to get the food for three meals a week?*

I thought of St. Mary's Soup Kitchen in Albany and the success of that facility. Lebanon was a town of 10,800, much smaller than Albany. *Would the community back this effort? Was the need really that great? If the people are there, would they come to a church for a meal?*

My mind began to cloud with doubts until the words from the public meeting resounded in my thoughts; "This is God's kitchen; let Him work out the details." Yes, this was the path that God wanted us to take.

God would work out the details just as He had when the multitude listening to Jesus grew hungry. His disciples wanted to send the 5000 men, plus women and children, away. Jesus replied, "They do not need to go away. You give them something to eat." The disciples answered, "We have here only five loaves of bread and two fish. Feeding them would take eight months of a man's wages!" (Matthew 14:16, 17; Mark 6:37)

Feeding the people who came to listen to Jesus was an insurmountable problem to His disciples. However, Jesus took what was available and "looking to heaven, He gave thanks." The need was filled.

When another 4000 men, plus women and children, following Jesus went three days without eating in order to learn from Him, He called his disciples and said, "I have compassion for these people." So with seven loaves and a few fish, the multitude "ate and was satisfied." (Matthew 15:32-39) Both times there were baskets full of food left.

The same question the disciples asked Jesus was now a concern for the compassionate volunteers; "How do we feed them?" The number needing to be fed was unknown. Jesus had not ignored the physical need for food during His ministry and He would not ignore it now.

There were many jobs to be done in the next month before a meal could be served. Marcy Huntsinger's gravelly voice read the list: write a business plan, fill out applications for assistance, file government forms, advertise for volunteers, set up schedules for volunteers, plan menus, gather food, up-grade wiring, and locate and purchase restaurant-sized pans, a warming table and other equipment.

The diverse chores sounded impossible. The disciples only needed food. The soup kitchen needed to meet regulations. The volunteers reminded themselves of the pledge made, "This is God's kitchen; let Him work out the details," and remained firm that the first meal would be served June 7, 1989.

I looked over the stack of legal forms, applications for grants and programs to receive discount food, paper items and cooking supplies. I didn't know where to start, but Dorothy Hull, director of St. Mary's Soup Kitchen, did. She quickly sorted papers into priorities, and helped Marcy fill them out. Soon the Lebanon Soup Kitchen was a legal non-profit organization.

We needed to ask the community for volunteers, donations of goods and money. Marcy and I wrote a flyer and sent it to newspapers, churches and organizations. Part of the flyer read, "The need is real. There are people in our community in need of a hot meal on a regular basis. Who are they? We don't know, and don't need to. We'll just provide good food at no charge." That simply stated our goal: to provide with no questions asked.

Dorothy Hull was director (and jack-of-all-trades, as she called it) of St. Mary's Soup Kitchen in Albany for ten years, beginning in 1982 when it opened. She told me of some of the obstacles she helped them overcome. "The state wanted to regulate us. They wanted to know where all participants came from and how many were children. They wanted to patrol in the soup kitchen for felons. At first they charged 25 cents to 50 cents to eat and people had to gather cans to get money. That was not the true spirit of a soup kitchen. I had to say 'no' to it all." Her soft voice was firm.

"Our first meal was soup and a big tub of lettuce. One woman said, 'All they need is a cup of soup and piece of bread.' That wouldn't be right if you were serving Jesus." Dorothy said. "If we had the food we should serve it. If we didn't serve it, what would we do with the excess?"

She looked under bridges or for families in cars. "I wanted to relieve some of their poverty by feeding them." Her concern spread beyond Albany as her wisdom and experience helped Lebanon, Keizer, Mt. Angel and other places start soup kitchens. Sharing her experience, Dorothy helped the Lebanon kitchen avoid some trial-and-error obstacles.

In Lebanon, Helen Richards volunteered her many years of experience in organizing. "Everything has to be efficient," she said, looking around the small working area of the kitchen. "Prep should use this back counter. They will be done before serving time so the biggest problem is going to be washing the dishes while serving. This area is going to be congested." She walked to the door leading into the dining hall, motioning along that area.

"We'll have to be careful," Marcy added, "but they should have enough room."

"We're getting day-old bread and desserts from Roth's," Hilda Blake's cheery voice interrupted with the announcement of successfully getting another business to donate their surplus. "I am going down to James-River to talk to them about paper products," she winked, knowing her infectious smile would persuade the paper company for help.

Between trips to various businesses to ask for whatever they could give, Hilda was ordering utensils and food from McDonalds and Quail Crest. She kept records on the government surplus cheese, butter and rice, along with donated items arriving. The 60-year-old's abundant energy flowed as encouragement for those around her.

As she was leaving, Bob Hauck announced, "Suburban Electric has the electrical panel installed." Bob was the handyman for the church and his job just expanded to include the Soup Kitchen. "The kitchen is ready as soon as the inspector approves it."

Marcy smiled in acknowledgement, "Great." She returned her attention to the kitchen. "Cooking here will work fine. What we need is storage."

"I'm working on that," Bob laughed, pointing toward the front of the church. "It's not close but I've added shelves in two closets in that front class room."

"We will take what we can get," Marcy said.

The news of the new soup kitchen began to spread and people began to call the First Christian Church for information, or to donate time or products. The church office was beyond the sanctuary from the kitchen. "Good morning, First Christian Church," Melva Hessevick, the church secretary, answered the phone. "Yes, the Soup Kitchen needs cooks," she said, picking up a pencil and sliding a note pad in front of her. "I can give your name to Marge Libra, who is scheduling them." She writes the information and thanks the caller. "This is why I went to the first meeting and am on the board," Melva explained. "I knew I would need to answer questions." She became one of the three volunteers to manage finances and keep records, a job she continued for 20 years.

To stop disturbing Melva's work for the church, a second phone line was installed in the kitchen. Most people called to offer their skills and time for cooking, serving, cleanup and laundry. But not all calls expressed delight with the plans. I answered several from angry people in the immediate neighborhood not wanting a soup kitchen near them. "You don't live near here, do you?" One lady snapped. "You wouldn't be doing this if you did." One caller huffed, "You should have seen the type of people that walked by my house today. You are bringing these people here by feeding them." A woman with a slow, sad voice pointed out, "You are fools for doing this. People will just take advantage of you."

My heart sank during the first call. It never occurred to me that there would be people against a soup kitchen. I could understand those who didn't want to be involved, but it was a surprise to hear the negative comments. *Would people, who aren't in financial need, come for a meal? Probably. We were giving a free meal and it was not our place to judge who took advantage of that. We welcomed everyone. Were we attracting more homeless or low-income people to come to Lebanon? We didn't know how many were here to begin with.*

I tried to calm their fears of a deteriorating neighborhood the best I could, but I had no foresight in what would happen. The invisible homeless were now becoming visible and their plight was being made known by establishing a way to meet at least one of their needs. *How would a soup kitchen affect the community? Would violence and crime increase? Were we putting our neighbors at higher risks?* There were no guarantees of what would happen, but to me the good that could be done far outweighed the possible threats.

"We are set to open as planned," Marcy announced to an enthralled board during their next meeting.

The community was coming together. Jesus answered the disciples with abundance; likewise the Soup Kitchen had all that was needed to feed the people, including eager volunteers.

Sample Menu:
Chicken Pot Pie
Corn
Green Salad
Fruit
Dessert

Fills Empty Plates

Start by doing what is necessary, then what's possible,
and suddenly you are doing the impossible.

Francis of Assisi

The smell of spaghetti sauce simmering in a large, stainless steel pot filled the crowded kitchen. The top of the domestic-sized stove bowed under the weight of the full pots. The cook and volunteer menu coordinator, Marge Libra carefully reached in the boiling water of one of the pots with a pair of prongs to pull out a noodle. It was ready. One of the men poured the pot into a strainer in the sink and rinsed the noodles before adding them to the sauce.

Marge and her friends, Helen Bellinger, Rose Duerr and Shirley Schmidt were preparing the first meal to be served at the Lebanon Soup Kitchen. Garlic bread warmed in the oven while the dressing was added to the green salad and bananas and strawberries were cut for dessert. Marcy Huntsinger, Hilda Blake, Von Hansen, Bob and Zee Hauck, I and others were setting out juice and milk, making coffee and double-checking that all was in order to serve the first patrons.

The sun shone brightly on a sidewalk sandwich board inviting people to come in. Part of it read "all are welcome" and "free meal." The colorful display was made by William West of Lebanon and painted by Cay Marshall of Sweet Home.

It was June 7, 1989. Excitement and nervousness filled the busy kitchen in anticipation of opening. Would there be enough food? Would people like it? Did we forget anything that should be done? Volunteers held hands in a circle for a prayer of blessing on the food, the preparers and the partakers.

Each went to their designated area to prepare for the guests gathering outside. Smiles passed between volunteers, acknowledging each others excitement. This was it. The doors were opened at the scheduled 5 p.m. serving time.

There was no line of people waiting. There was no one outside the doors or along the sidewalk. There was no one for the volunteers to serve. They looked at each other with long faces. Marcy walked to the sidewalk along the street, waiting for someone to come by for her to invite in. She didn't see anyone. "Maybe people are at the Strawberry Festival. It opened today," someone offered an explanation.

I walked through the church and found Pastor Doug Dornhecker in his office visiting with several people and invited them to join us. They were reluctant but I convinced them to please eat what we had spent so much time preparing. Others working around the church were also persuaded to enjoy the food. Finally, two carnival workers came in for a meal. At the end of the serving hour, we had fed about 15 people; most were volunteers who had come to serve. One volunteer said she couldn't eat because she felt as though she was taking food from those who needed it, even though they had not come to receive it.

The meal was prepared for 100. What could be frozen was placed in the upright freezer in the storage room on the other side of the church. The kitchen was cleaned, the floors mopped and the laundry taken home by someone to clean. The first night was complete.

I later visited with the local newspaper about the success of the first meal. "We are not discouraged but hope the program will build as more people hear about it," I told the reporter.

We were not discouraged because this was God's Kitchen and encouragement came from 2 Chronicles 15: 2b and 7; "The Lord is with you when you are with him. If you seek him, he will be found … be strong and do not give up, for your work will be rewarded."

The second night was similar to the first. The cooks, John and Helen Richards, worked all afternoon preparing tuna casserole with salad, fruit and dessert. Again, nearly a dozen volunteers arrived to help serve. Again, there was no line of guests at the door. Again, the meal was prepared for 100 but served only 15. The leftovers were frozen, the kitchen cleaned and volunteers went home.

Marcy was dissatisfied with the lack of attendance. "We aren't getting the word to the people who need it. Most of those who need the assistance don't read the paper that has written stories about us. We need more word-of-mouth." Her jaw sat firm with the strong determination that we had grown to recognize.

"I have a job for you," Marcy told Dirk, a homeless man who slept near the river. He grew up in Lebanon and knew many people. "Pass these flyers out around town." She handed him a stack of paper with an invitation for anyone to come to the Soup Kitchen.

In his ragged T-shirt and well-worn pants, Dirk greeted people with a cheerful smile as he walked around town in the spring sunshine, handing out flyers and talking about the soup kitchen. Many people saw the flyers and passed the invitation to others.

Over the weekend, the word had spread. Monday afternoon we received inquiries for information on our meals. A man called from Teen Challenge, a men's recovery program, saying about eight of them were coming. A lady from the Gleaners stopped by the kitchen to verify details so she could tell others.

For our third serving night, the cooks prepared for 100 guests.

When the doors opened at 5 p.m., guests were lined nearly to the street. Serving went smoothly until we realized we would run out of food. I began thawing the leftovers from the first two nights. Marcy went to the store for more milk and lettuce. Teen Challenge was waiting near the end of the line and we asked them to help. Some of the men began cutting lettuce for more salad. Others helped wash dirty dishes with bleach water and carried them in trays to the kitchen to run through a sterilizer. The cooks were warming anything in the pantry that was quick to fix. The dish washers had to squeeze by the servers with more clean plates for serving. People preparing salads had to squeeze by the dishwashers to get to the back counter. The cooks had to squeeze by those preparing foods to get to the stove. The servers had to squeeze by the cooks to get whatever was ready to serve. And squeeze we did, until everyone was fed. The last plates were a mix of what was available. Meatloaf was served with spaghetti noodles.

At 6 p.m. there was no one waiting to be served and we closed the doors. Instead of beginning cleanup, volunteers sat down with the men from Teen Challenge for a relaxing meal of whatever we could scrape together. Many told of their lives and how God had helped them better themselves through the Teen Challenge program. Volunteers also shared stories of how God worked in their lives. Everyone was thankful how God provided to feed so many people, even the volunteers. What may have been chaos to us, God turned into a successful evening.

That night set the pace for what became the average guest count.

People came for different reasons. Some were invited through the Senior Center or Gleaners. Some were homeless. Others had a place to live but needed the help for their paycheck to last all month. Some were lonely and needed the social interaction. The reason didn't matter.

Marcy explained her views in an article in the Lebanon Express, "If a family should eat with us for a week and thereby save enough money to go to a restaurant, or a movie, or buy food for a special dinner at home, I think that may be good for business in Lebanon, good for the family, and a good use of a small part of our time and work. If we can find a way to communicate with the poorest of the poor – the homeless – and they come to eat with us, I think that may be good for them and for our world."

How many needed a place to eat a warm meal? More than we thought. We started doing what we thought we could but that evening showed we could also do the impossible.

Sample Menu:
Chile
Cornbread
Green Salad
Fruit
Dessert

A Mixing of Gifts

What does love look like? It has the hands to help others.
It has the feet to hasten to the poor and needy.
It has the eyes to see misery and want.
It has the ears to hear the sighs and sorrows of men.
That is what love looks like.

St. Augustine

"Do you know how to tell if someone doesn't have any friends?" I asked a volunteer while washing zucchini which had been left at the Soup Kitchen door.

"No." The volunteer's forehead furrowed curious of the question.

"They buy zucchini." I laughed at the joke about the abundance of the long, green squash found in local gardens. One vine can produce enough for a family, plus a surplus to give away.

Her face relaxed with a smile as we looked at the box full of the vegetable.

"We must have a lot of friends."

An article about the Soup Kitchen in the June 7, 1989, issue of the *Lebanon Express* stated, "Kitchen organizers ask local residents to plant an extra row in their garden this summer and donate the vegetable from the row." Many people heeded the challenge and boxes of fruits and vegetables began arriving at the Soup Kitchen. Large, red tomatoes, crisp green beans, ears of corn, fresh heads of lettuce and lots of zucchini added to the Soup Kitchen's larder.

Cooks became creative in using zucchini. They were fried with tomatoes, boiled or stuffed. A favorite casserole was zucchini with meat, peppers, onions, tomatoes and covered with cheese. The only limit was the cook's imagination.

When shiny, red apples arrived, Helen, who cooked with her husband, John, would fry some. "Everyone seems to like it and one lady told me it was just like her grandmother used to make," Helen said.

Bev Copeland and Dorothy Page were regular cooks who were flexible in using the donations. "I cook like I do for my family," Bev told me one afternoon. "The onion bread is good with meatballs and the white bread is good as pudding or custard. Cabbage is good with tomatoes and Walla-Walla onions." She laughed, "One time I cooked the three together and people drank the juice from the bowls."

John Puma grew an organic garden at his home. "I give what I can and am glad to help. One year I gave ten percent of my produce and was proud to do so." He spoke of his respect for the Soup Kitchen. "It's wonderful that it is there but it's a tragedy that it is needed."

Food was never allowed to go to waste. Excess amounts were shared with the guests or The Lord's Storehouse, a place that gave out food boxes twice a week.

People who didn't have gardens gave in their own way. One gentleman spent $20-$50 each week on sale items at local grocery stores. Another man spent ten percent of his income on food to give to the Soup Kitchen.

Local dairies gave meat, while the Soup Kitchen or a volunteer paid for the cut and wrap. Individuals and businesses purchased a steer or hog at the annual 4-H Livestock auction to donate.

One school collected canned food to donate while another had a scavenger hunt to gather food. The Lebanon Community Concert held a benefit performance in the sanctuary of the First Christian Church.

One lady loved to shop store sales. She brought new clothes to hand out.

Two dentists raised money through giving special discounts to patients.

The Soup Kitchen "is one of the main arteries of helping those in need in our community," Bev Copeland said. "It is a city-wide project and has made a great impact in the community. God means for us to help and treat them (the needy) with dignity."

Many community businesses were generous in contributing. Roth's IGA Foodliner, Lebanon Shop N Kart and Stiffler's each donated day-old breads and pastries. Big Towne Hero increased the amount of bread it made each morning to assure there would be loaves left for the Soup Kitchen. Easy Breeze Café donated soup while Burger King gave coupons to be handed out to guests. One-Thousand Villages designated days in which a percentage of their sales went to the Soup Kitchen. Etcetera Shop made clothes available for people from the Soup Kitchen. When fresh fruits and vegetables were out of season Monarch Travel purchased some. Several restaurants donated surplus food from catered dinners. Four salons in town gave coupons for haircuts. Willamette Valley Rehabilitation Center built pallets to keep items off the floor in a storage room.

Three dairies supported with their products. Mallories Dairy gave a huge discount on milk and delivered it to Roth's IGA Foodliner for someone from the Soup Kitchen to easily pick up. Timber Valley Dairy also contributed milk for a time.

John Volbeda from Volbeda Dairy in Albany gave meat. When he first gave, he had cows butchered and the Soup Kitchen or a supporter paid the cut and wrap. When meat was needed, Volbeda could be counted on for a donation. Over the years, he began paying for the cut and wrap and called the Soup Kitchen when the meat was ready to pick up.

At board meetings unanimous gratitudes were written to businesses. Besides the above, others were: Sprouce!, Red Beard's Steak and Seafood Restaurant, D&K Market, Franz Bakery, James River Corp., Tak Yuen Chinese American Restaurant, R-Place and Canaga Tire.

When Wal-Mart closed their old store in 2005, they donated 150 pounds of food and at the Grand Opening of the new store they gave the Soup Kitchen $2,000.

Organizations joined in helping. Altrusa Club sponsored a children's reading area at one end of the dining hall. Two bookcases of reading material, puzzles and a child-size table and chairs made up the "Book Nook." They also prepared Easter baskets. Rotary Club gave $500 and challenged other organizations to meet that. Compassionate Friends would pick up homeless and take them to an Albany Shelter. American Legion held a Beef Stew Dinner and a Chili Feed as benefits to the Soup Kitchen. St. Vincent De Paul, Gleaners, Senior Center, Elks Lodge, Kiwanis, Modern Woodmen of America and Salvation Army were part of giving.

Many local churches became involved. Southside Church of Christ donated personal care kits which were available to hand out as needed. Church of God gave blankets. The Presbyterian Church gave tomato juice. The Lutheran Brotherhood requested a grocery list for them to purchase $200 a month of needed items. St. Edwards Catholic church also brought food, and several churches' youth groups came to serve.

One church's primary Sunday school children collected money in "hungry jars." Once a month, they brought it to the Soup Kitchen and sang for the volunteers as they presented their gifts. "They were very special," one volunteer smiled when telling me of the group.

The Awana Club at Lebanon First Baptist Church donated part of their "penny wars" to the Soup Kitchen. They had a collection jar for the boys and one for the girls. When a penny was added they received a positive count but if a silver coin was added they received a negative count. Boys would add their silver coins to the girls jar and vice versa. The collection was divided among several charities.

When some of the guests were asking for needle and thread for clothing repairs, Melva, the Soup Kitchen treasurer, took the problem to her quilter's group. The ladies at Our Savior's Lutheran Church made sewing kits which included needles, thread, buttons and pins.

St. Martin's Episcopal Church set a table at the Soup Kitchen to hand out personal care kits and toiletry items several times a year. The kits included a wash cloth, toothbrush and paste, shampoo, lotions and a comb. They were placed in gallon Ziploc bags with a picture of Jesus and a prayer. Extra items, of which guests could choose three, were bathroom tissue, shampoo, men's or women's deodorant or razors. "Most choose the TP," Helen, a volunteer, laughed as she showed me the kits. "Diapers and women's sanitary items are given out when asked for."

Other fundraisers were a Golf Scramble in 1993 and the sale of calendars with Soup Kitchen photographs in 2007.

Warm clothing left from a rummage sale was shared with the Yakima Christian Indian Mission at Toppenish, Wash. Marge Libra worked hard on the sale and sending the leftovers. "It recycled a lot of good, used clothing," she boasted.

The generosity shown the Soup Kitchen has been extended to others with the interest earned from its bank accounts. They provided spaghetti and meat sauce for a Habitat for Humanity Spaghetti Feed and served a spaghetti feed for a Homeless Shelter fundraiser. For several years, a fund was kept to pay for one-night rooming at a local motel in emergency cases. A Thanksgiving box was prepared one year for a family in need of a meal.

Following Hurricane Katrina, they donated $2500 toward its recovery efforts through Church World Service. According to Church World Service website, part of the note accompanying the check read, "On behalf of the Christian community in Lebanon, the board members for the Lebanon Soup Kitchen voted to make a contribution to the Hurricanes Katrina and Rita relief fund...The funds received are from church members, and many loyal donors, but mostly from God."

The work of the Soup Kitchen has seen many blessings and can be seen in the description given in Deuteronomy 15:10 -11; "Give generously to him and do so without a grudging heart; then because of this the Lord your God will bless you in all your work and in everything you put your hand to. There will always be poor people in the land. Therefore I command you to be openhanded toward your brothers and toward the poor and needy in your land."

The above volunteers may have contributed more than I have mentioned. Others have given but are not recognized here. Each one who contributed in any way, whether mentioned or not, is greatly appreciated.

The Soup Kitchen truly has many friends who hear the needs of the poor. Those friends have made the Soup Kitchen an integral part of the community, bringing people together for an important cause. The generous and giving hearts of individuals, businesses, organizations and churches are a picture of what love looks like.

Sample Menu:
Beef and Rice Casserole
Beans
Green Salad
Fruit
Dessert

Culinary Artists

The bread of charity is holy bread which the praise
and the love of the Lord God sanctifies.

St. Francis of Assissi

A cook is defined as "one who prepares food." To cook is "to devise or invent." The cooks at the Soup Kitchen often devise or invent a meal from available ingredients. Cooks, who usually donate one day a month, are creative as well as skilled in their culinary achievements.

The menu is scheduled in advance, but when perishable food arrives the cook may need to make adjustments. The menu remains flexible in order to assure the best use of the donated food. Prepared foods have been brought following catered meals from restaurants and from the culinary departments at OSU and Linn Benton Community College. Often, these must be served immediately, leaving the cooks to abandon their original plans.

When I asked several cooks for the recipe of their favorite dishes, I was met with laughter. "We use what comes in. It may be a little different each time," Gisela, a cook, explained. "The recipes are up here," she said, tapping on her head.

"Stone Soup is our recipe," Martha, Gisela's cooking partner, added, referring to the old tale.

Preparing a meal can be an artistic endeavor. Some plan their special entrée with care, bringing their own ingredients to assure the flavor they want. Others, like Gisela and Martha, see what is available and create a recipe around it.

One of those was Mary Sanders. "She created some of the best stuff from what was in the refrigerator." Zee, co-manager said. "She cooked by taste, not recipes. She was careful not to use too much salt because it wasn't good for some people." She also worked to keep the food healthy by removing fat from gravy by carefully laying paper towels on the top to soak it up.

Years before, when Mary's husband retired from his job in the South, the couple moved to Lebanon. At that time Mary wanted a job working outside her home, but the only skill she knew was cooking for church potlucks and PTA events. Using those talents, she became employed for the first time in her life by cooking at Pineway Restaurant & Golf Course. Later she took courses in commercial cookery. She worked at several other restaurants around the mid-valley and Portland, finishing her career at the Tom-Tom Restaurant in Albany. Usually, she worked for other proprietors but for a time she owned The Chili Bowl in Lebanon.

One day, after retiring, she saw a sign at a laundromat asking for cooks at the Soup Kitchen. She didn't hesitate to volunteer her time and knowledge. She brought her own knives to use and never allowed them to be placed in hot, soapy water because she insisted that would dull them.

"She had remedies for everything from cooking errors to health issues," said Joyce, co-manager.

I learned that was true when I complained of sinus problems. Mary told me to drink hot water with vinegar and honey. But the honey must be from nectar of the plant I was sensitive to. I starting drinking the mixture and found I felt much better.

Mary was 92 years old before she stopped preparing meals for the needy.

Zee, one of the original volunteers, helped other cooks until she felt comfortable cooking on her own. Her first day as the main cook, she remained nervous but with the help of Dirk, a volunteer, she felt things were going smoothly. The two stirred packages of Jell-O in pots of hot water and poured the liquid into long, stainless steel pans. They carefully slid the pans in the refrigerator to chill. Before they started their next project, the refrigerator door flew open and the pans of warm liquid crashed to the floor splashing Jell-O across the kitchen. Green streaks lined the cabinet doors and dotted the lower shelves.

The sticky substance jelled before Zee and Dirk could scrub it from all the places it oozed into. They cleaned the rest of the afternoon in between preparing the meal. The broken shelf in the refrigerator was quickly repaired but the "Jell-O incident" will always be Zee's memory of how she started as a cook.

Dirk often helped Zee and was eager to start preparations while Zee gathered ingredients. One afternoon, he had several kettles filled with boiling water and added nearly a pound of oregano leaves and other spices. Soup was scheduled on the menu for the evening meal but there was far more water and spice than what was needed. "He was so proud of himself, I couldn't dump it out," Zee shook her head. "I just used what I could."

A smile lit her fair face when she talked of the volunteers. "The cooks were all different. One cooked with a lot of rosemary. Another made spicy meals. But meals were always good. Some had to be dressed up, but they all came out perfect."

Zee spent 13 years cooking and co-managing the Soup Kitchen. When one of the cooks asked her why she and Bob, her husband, gave so many hours, she explained in her soft, gentle voice, "Well, it is our mission."

Zee was a long-time resident of Lebanon and knew a wide range of people. Few escaped her request to help at the Soup Kitchen. Zee donated much of her time working at the Soup Kitchen but one year wanted time to spend Christmas with her family. She asked her friends, Dr. Patrick R. Burkett and his wife, Alvila, to serve for her during the holidays. They gladly agreed and brought their friends, Walt and Marielu Eager. That began eight years of service as the two couples drove from Corvallis once a month to prepare a meal.

"I was impressed with the Soup Kitchen volunteers. They had a real desire to serve," Alvila said.

Another friend who Zee often asked to help was Gisela Zerkel. She told Zee that she would help at the Soup Kitchen if she didn't already have a job. "The ink was not dry on my last paycheck when Zee called to see when I could volunteer," Gisela laughed, recalling how she started at the Soup Kitchen.

"I went to get my food license and as soon as the people giving the test heard that I already cooked at the Soup Kitchen, they handed me my license," Gisela said in her thick German accent. "The reputation of the Soup Kitchen is such that others know that rules are strictly enforced here.

"There is a lot of gratification in serving," Gisela acknowledged, but reflected on a sad story that deeply affected her. "Some servers give larger portions than others. One had dished a large amount on a plate for a child. I asked the little boy with big, brown eyes if he could eat that much. He said that he hadn't eaten all day and he would clean it up." She hesitated with a heavy sigh. "I told him to come back if he needed more."

Not long after Gisela began cooking, she convinced her long-time friend, Martha Biederbeck, that she needed her help. The two prepared meals twice a month until the summer of 2007, when Gisela broke her pelvis. Martha carried on until Gisela could return.

The anniversary of the opening of the Soup Kitchen was cause for celebration. Each year the community was invited to join the Soup Kitchen for a picnic. Jack and Janine LaFranchise would bring their large grill fixed on a trailer and cook hamburgers and hot dogs in the parking lot. Tables were set up beneath the trees at the end of the building. Salads, chips and desserts were served, along with drinks. Publicity for the celebration was a reminder to the community of the service being provided and the need for support.

The picnic was only a small part of Jack and Janine's dedication. They cooked once a month for 13 years and helped make the special Christmas dinner possible after its creator, Frank Crowley died.

Webb came to Lebanon in July 2007 looking for a place "small enough that in day-to-day life you would run into someone you know or someone who knows someone you know." After choosing Lebanon, he began looking for a place to volunteer, not only to serve but to learn about the people who live and care about their community.

All of this was for a year-long study in working toward his PhD in Demography. He lived in Eugene with his wife, who studied at U of O for her masters in History Preservation.

The Soup Kitchen was not the only place Webb found to volunteer. He did tutoring and helped in the game room at the Lebanon Boys & Girls Club and taught computer skills at Community Services Consortium (CSC). "This is a boot-strap community," he told me one afternoon, during a break from cooking. "The community knows how to organize and pull itself up.

"One of the things I care about a great deal is the Soup Kitchen. It impresses me with such a large effort for a small town. Half the people each night are the same guests." He looked around the now-empty dining hall and nodded toward a group of volunteers gathered near the kitchen. "There is a lot of emotion in it. If there wasn't then they shouldn't be doing it. People are sometimes too proud. Some won't come here but should. We need to find a way around that."

Webb cooked at the Soup Kitchen once a month and helped serve on other occasions. This was his first experience in cooking for more than 10-20 family members at Thanksgiving dinner. Two favorite meals he served were Mexican fiesta and spaghetti, both excellent.

A guest told me one night while eating his second helping, "I have been to a lot of places that give meals. They have the best food here."

The cooks served meals in accordance with the words Jesus spoke to His host in Luke 14: 12-14, "When you give a luncheon or dinner, do not invite your friends, your brothers or relatives, or your rich neighbors; if you do they may invite you back and so you will be repaid. But when you give a banquet invite the poor, the crippled, the lame, the blind, and you will be blessed. Although they cannot repay you, you will be repaid at the resurrection of the righteous."

I have introduced you to only a few of the gourmet artists who praised and loved God by serving the bread of charity.

Sample Menu:
Spaghetti
Green Beans
Green Salad
Applesauce

Salt of the Earth

*The best and most beautiful things cannot be seen
or touched – they must be felt with the heart.*

Helen Keller

A plaque on the wall in the dining room is titled "Lebanon Soup Kitchen Remembers." There are six names engraved on it. Each brought his own special gift in serving others.

Ed Merzenich was one of the first to volunteer, along with his wife, Edna. Their optimism helped secure donors and volunteers when the Soup Kitchen was being established. The elderly couple gathered donations and helped in preparation of meals. Edna was allergic to lettuce and had to be careful when it was served. Her hands would swell if she handled anything that had touched lettuce.

Ed was a tall, slender man who loved his rose garden. He was proud to share his flowers and brightened each table in the dining hall with a rose. His cheerfulness and dedication was cut short by declining health. His death in 1990 brought the Soup Kitchen family the first encounter with the death of one of their own. In remembrance of his short time with us, a plaque was made in his honor. Beneath his name is inscribed, "He brought roses."

Other names were added over the years.

Hilda and Wayne Blake were dedicated from the moment they attended the planning meeting. Hilda's age had not slowed her boundless energy as she combed the community for donations or searched for good buys on food and supplies. Her bright eyes and radiant smile were a welcome presence in the busy kitchen. "She was a gift from God." said Joyce, a volunteer.

Wayne passed away in 1993. At that time both their names were added to the plaque referring to them as "God's Secret Agents." When Hilda died in 1995, her name was added again with the inscription, "She made a difference in many lives." That she did.

One of the founders of the Soup Kitchen, Marcy Huntsinger, left us forever in 1995. Beneath her name are the simple words, "She knew it could be done." Her dedication and determination never wavered in her commitment to serve the needy. She stood as a solid example and she stirred up the community to see her vision.

Marcy not only gave as a volunteer, she helped to improve people's lives at her job as a speech therapist. Most of her clients were stroke victims who needed assistance in re-learning to talk. Her compassion was evident everywhere in her life.

"She was not a person of wealth," said Joyce, a volunteer who worked with Marcy for several years. "She was a hard worker. I remember her crawling in cupboards to get pots and pans."

She became an example to others in her giving. One of those was an early volunteer, Lorin Dante. He talked affectionately while remembering his friend and mentor. "She was fervent in her quest to help others. She had heart and was strong. She had convictions and stuck to them." He explained her gift of giving. "She gave because she was a giver. It was her state of being. She didn't give in drops but in buckets."

Her perseverance and persistence in bringing food to the needy brought together many people. Her enthusiasm was contagious, inspiring volunteers to give of their time and talents. Her vision became a community vision with support to carry the work for years.

Doris Mesecher was welcomed in September 1989 as the first volunteer to co-ordinate the Community Services workers. She handled all the paperwork for those serving at the Soup Kitchen as part of their time denoted by the court. The position was hard to fill and her efforts were greatly appreciated. Besides keeping the Community Services records, she often took the nightly count or helped in other areas.

Doris spent her life as a homemaker and raised five children. She never learned to drive but was active in a local organization. She met a man at one of the meetings who worked at the Soup Kitchen. He suggested she volunteer her cooking skills. A neighbor on the next block, Marcy Huntsinger, also asked if she would be willing to help. When a third friend encouraged her to help, she decided maybe she should give it a try.

For four years, Doris was at the Soup Kitchen three times a week for three to four hours each day. As her health began to fail, her attendance became sporadic. She gave up the Community Service recordkeeping but continued to help when her health allowed.

When she passed away in 1998, her name was added to the plaque. She is remembered as "a giver, not a taker with the heart."

Sylvia Voll learned to drive after her husband died so that she could get to the Soup Kitchen. "She was a sweetheart who you could always count on being there," said one volunteer. For several years she took the guest count or worked in serving. The plaque describes her as "a faithful and dedicated servant."

The last name was added in 2002 when Frank Crowley died. He was a hearty man with an infectious smile who had a gentle touch in serving an elegant meal. His efforts to make Christmas dinner special brought an extra joy to the holidays for many who may not ever be treated to such delicacy. He was known for his special touch at Christmas but he was busy behind the scene with a dream to build an addition on the kitchen.

The inscription beneath his name reads, "His love for the hungry, the homeless, the soup kitchen, and his special Christmas dinners will never be forgotten." Neither will his generous giving of himself.

These are only six of the hundreds of volunteers to support the Soup Kitchen over the years. They are examples of Paul's reminder in Acts 20:35, "I showed you that by this kind of hard work we must help the weak, remembering the words the Lord Jesus himself said: 'It is more blessed to give than to receive.'"

Many have left fond memories with those they touched. Not all the "angels" who have blessed the Soup Kitchen with their giving are deceased. If all their names were listed on plaques, the walls of the dining room would be covered. Even though there are no decorative wall hangings to commemorate each of them, the Soup Kitchen remembers what is felt in the heart.

Sample Menu:
Ham
Mashed Potatoes
Peas
Green Salad
Peaches
Dessert

Kitchen Utensils

Being a volunteer is one of the best things you can do
with your life.
Blessings were worth more than any amount of money
anyone could pay me.

Dorothy Hull, St. Mary's Soup Kitchen

In "The City That Friendliness Built," as the sign at the end of town states, hundreds of volunteers have served in the Soup Kitchen in many different capacities. Cooking and serving are more visible jobs than washing laundry or picking up donations. But each one fills a need and adds to the success of the whole.

Service is not given to draw attention to individuals. As Jesus told us in Matthew 6:1 and 4, "When you give a gift to someone in need, don't shout about it as the hypocrites do…give your gifts in secret, and your Father, who knows all secrets, will reward you."

It is the heart that makes the action a gift of humble service. The reward does not require any acknowledgement from man. However, I would like you to meet some of the givers, who did not ask to have your attention. One example is a man who wanted to do more than fill stomachs, but to fill lives with a moment of warmth.

The Optimist Club volunteered to prepare and serve meals on a Monday night once a month. Jim McDaniels was president at that time. He started washing dishes and later moved to serving. He was a big man but never complained about the cramped area of the small kitchen. When the club stopped volunteering as a group, Jim remained a constant figure at the serving table. The retired teacher and coach filled that spot each Monday night for ten years.

"Everyone has a responsibility to give back to the community in which they work," he told me one day while visiting in his office. "I don't work there because it's noble. I do it for a selfish reason. When I was young I was told that it was better to give than to receive. I never understood as a child but I really understand serving in that line. When I am there I focus on what they need. I make them my focus, I try to make them laugh or smile."

It wasn't only the guests who felt his encouraging persona. His easy-going attitude is contagious among the other volunteers.

Jim joked that he was second spoon in the serving line, similar to the musician in an orchestra working his way to the coveted first chair. The cook usually dished up the main course which was served first. Jim was next, or second spoon. Eventually, he felt promoted when he became first spoon.

While he served the main dish, one guest told him, "We like it when you're here, the food tastes so much better. You're such a good cook." Jim never cooked.

"It was how the food was presented and served," the soft spoken man explained. "It was a darn good atmosphere. I would sing and say, "If you've got a quarter I will stop," or "How much would you give me to not sing?" It was all in fun."

Jim was a big man and piled the food high on plates. "The people come here because they are hungry." Others were concerned that Jim's generosity could result in possibly running out of food or too much being thrown out.

John Richards defended the large shares. "Unless you've been hungry, you can't know what it means to have more than you need. We never ran out of food or turned anyone away."

Jim's greatest pleasure was serving at the Soup Kitchen. "Not many will stand up for the downtrodden." Like the orchestra with its rows of musicians, the Soup Kitchen volunteers serve in all areas to deliver a soothing atmosphere, as well as food. It was just as much joy for Jim to wash dishes as it was to become first spoon. It is better to play second fiddle than not make music with the orchestra at all.

As a business owner with 200 employees, he had the means to try to solve each guest's problem. "It's hard not to give them money. But I know that is not the best way to help."

The atmosphere he brought to the Soup Kitchen did not go unnoticed by those he served. When Jim went on a long vacation, some of the guests asked about him. His hearty laugh and big smile were truly missed.

Another volunteer whose quiet presence was appreciated by the guests was Majel Tracy. Beginning in 2002, she sat at one end of the long table that held the trays and silverware. As the guests went through the serving line, she tallied each one. Children were counted separate from adults. Seconds and food taken home were also marked separately. Some nights there would be as many as 150 guests while other nights may only have 40 or 50.

"We meet a lot of nice people," she once told me. Later, she learned how right she was. While working in her garden at home, she fell and bruised several ribs, keeping her from working at the Soup Kitchen.

While she recovered, I took her place in tallying. Many people asked where she was or how she was doing. I would report each night that she was improving. One evening a guest, Arnie, told me he was going to get a card for her. Sure enough, the next evening he arrived with a get-well card. I left it on the table in front of me for people to sign as they waited in line. The card was nearly covered with signatures when it was later given to Majel.

When daylight fades early during the winter months, Majel couldn't stay to take the count. She spent the afternoons helping to prepare for serving but had to drive home while there is still light enough for her failing eyes to focus on the road. In the spring, she returned to her chair for counting.

Failing eyesight, also, lead another volunteer to stop coming after years of service. Doris Smith come every Monday, Wednesday and Friday at 1:30 p.m. and stayed until the cleanup was finished. However, she only began after her grandson, Tony Mosso, brought her to the Soup Kitchen. Tony stayed with Doris following her husband's funeral and was eager to help when he learned of the Soup Kitchen. Tony trained at the prestigious Culinary Institute of American in Hyde Park, N.Y., and in France, Italy and Spain. He worked with the cooks in preparing meals while Doris found other ways to help. She seldom missed a day of serving wherever she was needed, until she lost her eyesight.

Another area adding to the orchestra of the Soup Kitchen is the, well, the music.

In the back of the dining hall there is a mini-grand piano belonging to the church. Paul Landrus was an accomplished pianist who came for a short period of time. "It lifted the peoples' spirits," Joyce, a retired music teacher, cooed. "Paul played the piano smooth and gentle, not overpowering. He does have a God-given touch." Her smile broadened as she recalled his music. "He played old-time gospel, country western or whatever came to his mind. One day he brought his guitar and began playing hymns during the meal. All who were familiar with them joined in and nearly everyone was singing. It brought a joyous atmosphere."

Music was brought on Friday's by Norma McPherson who enjoyed the chance to play. At Christmas, Ray Hendricks, retired music teacher, graciously shared his talents while a few guests sang along to the season's melodies.

Not all the music has been during the meal. One volunteer, Bruce, brought his son and friends to play a concert in the sanctuary following dinner. Several guests joined others from the community for the rock band's performance.

On a different note that added a new light to the dining hall was Alborz Monjazeb, who was walking across America on Highway 20, from Newport, Oregon to Boston, Massachusetts. His 'Walk for Progress' was for personal growth, to develop a Web site and to gather donations for small projects in the communities he passed through. To explore different American experiences, his walk through Lebanon brought him to the Soup Kitchen to help as well as eat. He wrote in his journal on his Website, "these are not "soup" meals but rather full nutritional home-cooked dinners of lasagna, salad, bread, fruits, juices, desserts of various sorts and great dining services! I was fortunate to be able to help out bussing tables and cleaning up as dozens of families came for meals and there was plenty for everyone to have seconds. I enjoyed my meal very much."

Joyce Dart and Zee Hauck, coordinators of the Soup Kitchen, wrote a letter to the editor of the Lebanon Express in 2001. It stated, "this community is so fortunate to have people who are very caring. The volunteers who come in to cook, serve and clean come with a willing heart to make a difference…You all need to know how much you are appreciated. Thank you." The appreciation is felt as strongly today, encompassing many more willing hearts.

Whether the job is washing pots, counting guests or playing music, each has an equal part of the melody orchestrated by the volunteers to make the best music of their lives.

Sample Menu:
Baked Salmon
Baked Potatoes
Carrots
Fresh Fruit Salad
Gelatin
Blueberry Shortcake
Ice Cream

Flavors of Spice

No one is useless in the world who lightens the burden of it
for anyone else.

Charles Dickens

V olunteers give of their time and gifts as a demonstration of the love
that Jesus implored us to have for one another. The apostle John
tells us, "Dear Children, let us stop saying that we love each other; let us
really show it by our actions." (I John 3:18 New Living Translation) Love
is shown by using that which we have to benefit others. The following
are some of those love stories.

Marge Stevens, a retired hairdresser, volunteered to cut hair in the church
foyer on Wednesdays. She set up with a chair, clippers, brush, a black drape
and disinfectant for her tools. "The people had to have a clean head in order
to get a haircut. I had quite a few to cut. I preferred trimming but would
cut any length and I always swept up afterwards," she explained. "I enjoyed
doing it. They would talk and I could get to know them. I learned a lot about
them. One man was dying of cancer and I gave him his last hair cut."

She laughed about a time when the electricity went off. "I was half done
with a man's hair. He had thick, coarse, curly hair. I tried finishing with scissors
but it wasn't good." Marge's thin face blushed. "I always cut his kids hair, too.
He had a big family. Then there was a man who had a strange hairline with a
cowlick in front." She made a swirl with her finger at the top of her forehead.
"It was hard to get it right but he kept coming back so he must have liked it."

Marge gave up her "salon" at the "country club" when her health began
to fail. She and her husband, Roy, often returned to the Soup Kitchen for a
meal and to fellowship with friends they have made.

XXXXX

Keith found part of his past after him and his wife, Marcia, came to the Soup Kitchen. The devastating closure of their sole propriety business was not due to their lack of skill or management but through eminent domain. With their source of income gone, they could no longer make their house payments and soon lost their home. After a few visits to eat at the Soup Kitchen, they volunteered to help.

Keith was depressed about their circumstances but confided he always had a sad spot in his heart for his father, a Vietnam POW he never knew. He was too young to remember his father when he went off to war. His mother and family members would not talk about his father, as though he never existed. Curiosity about the man he longed to know left a hole that was never filled.

A chance meeting at the Soup Kitchen became an answer to Keith's life-long prayer. They were helping prepare Thanksgiving turkeys when they met Ron and Nancy VanVleet. Both Marcia and Keith felt their connecting was by the grace of God. Ron and Nancy were substituting for the regular driver, delivering bread and pastry from local stores. During a casual conversation, the four learned that Nancy went to high school with Keith's father. She told him all about the man she knew growing up. The picture she gave of his father helped heal the sadness Keith had kept through the years.

XXXXX

Lorin Dante held a special place in his heart for the Soup Kitchen and his opportunity to help there. He grew up and graduated from high school in Lebanon, but his journey led him to many places. During a visit to Lebanon while unemployed, he met Marcy. She was working hard to establish the Soup Kitchen and eagerly accepted his help in cooking, cleaning, serving and picking up donations.

"Marcy gave to everyone, unconditionally. We could use some more people like Marcy. She was strong and helped the weak. She gave birth to some of my energy." Lorin told me as I studied his artwork covering his living room wall. "Marcy will never leave me. It was a blessing to have the time with her. She touched many lives. So has the Soup Kitchen." He motioned for me to sit on the leather couch along another wall filled with his art.

He pulled a chair closer to the couch and relaxed into its firmness and explained the love he had for a place he visited a couple of times a year. "Acceptance is a big thing. You don't know what little thing can draw someone back into life. Other places that offer food, talk about condemnation, sin and changing lifestyles but here these are people of God. They have a lilt, a shine in their voice. Jesus did a lot of doing. If you do good things, other people see it. That is what this Soup Kitchen does." He returned twice a year to Lebanon Soup Kitchen to soak in the atmosphere and be reminded what he received from many people like Marcy.

He also had fond memories of helping others while serving at the Corvallis Soup Kitchen. "One night I was serving and looked up at the familiar face of a man, John, who I served at the Salvation Army in Santa Barbara. He didn't remember me until we got to talking. He was looking for a job. I used my network and the guy had a job in two weeks." He raised a tall glass of cold water to his lips. The drink was refreshing reprieve in the afternoon heat.

"While I was in Corvallis, I would go to the park on Saturdays and let anyone use my phone to call someone. That line of communication was helpful. One couple got back together after being able to talk."

XXXXX

Steve was at a low point in his life when he came to the Soup Kitchen. He worked a full-time job and attended classes for Computer Information Technology. When he was laid off, he could no longer take classes. He struggled to pay his bills. The Soup Kitchen offered him a warm meal when he didn't have one.

To show his appreciation for the food, Steve helped clean dishes during the meals. Soon he saw a way to help others and came to set up, join in the prayer circle and work wherever needed. Whether he served, carried trays, or cleaned during meals, he always mopped floors and was one of the last to leave.

Steve lived six miles from the Soup Kitchen and spent one and a half years riding his bicycle when his car broke down. Steve worked odd jobs for people and eventually was able to buy another car. He faithfully came and brought Chuck, a neighbor in the trailer park where he lived. Soon Chuck was as committed as Steve in serving each night.

Another volunteer who rode his bicycle was Michael. Each Wednesday the dark-haired youth rode or walked from Lebanon High School, where he was a sophomore, to the Soup Kitchen in all sorts of weather. His father picked him up or a volunteer took him the four miles home if the weather was too bad. When asked why he served, he shrugged his shoulders and softly replied, "Because I want to."

Other students volunteered with wiping tables or cleaning plates as extra credit for their health class at the Lebanon High School. Eric Mock didn't stop volunteering when he finished the health project but returned often while in high school and later when he was home from college. He wrote to the editor of the Lebanon Express, "Besides making a difference in the lives of others, the Soup Kitchen has also made a difference in my own life…Through many experiences at the Soup Kitchen I have seen that I would like to work more with the needy as I get older. Although I am unsure where this may take me, I have made up my mind that I would like to continue volunteering."

Travas Keith, 15, encouraged his friend, Jeff Sizemore, to serve for a day at the Soup Kitchen in lieu of a book assignment in health class in 1995. Jeff was embarrassed to go. "No one will know," Travas assured him. That was almost true. No one knew except the thousands of people who read the Albany Democrat-Herald and saw the boys' picture as part of a full-page article about the Soup Kitchen.

"We were heckled at school after that, but in a fun way," Jeff laughed. "We did it to get out of the classroom. It was the first time I had seen people who needed that help. It was alarming to see so many. This is a small town, I saw a man my dad knew and we were both uncomfortable. There was one of my relatives in line but he left. I don't think he ever knew that I saw him."

Not all volunteers were local or even state residents. Betty and Paul Lane from Missouri came to Lebanon to visit her brother. The couple served many meals during their vacation.

One who brought more comfort with her warm presence than any skill was Angela. She was mentally handicapped but eager to help when the Soup Kitchen first sought volunteers. Her crooked smile lit her round face and her green eyes shined with pride as she rubbed a towel in circles around the tables. "She just made people feel good," one cook said.

Each one has lightened the load for someone else in their own special way.

Sample Menu:
BBQ Chicken
Baked Potatoes
Carrots and Peas
Green Salad
Dessert

Courtesy of Zee Hauck
Eric Mook washing trays.

Blends the Work

Let no one ever come to you without leaving better and happier.

Mother Teresa

The Soup Kitchen operated with only volunteer help for 12 years. Joyce Dart and Zee Hauck donated hundreds of hours in co-managing all of the functions. Their efforts allowed the Soup Kitchen to exist and offer assistance to many people. But they needed someone to officially manage the daily operations. It was time for a paid manager to take over. The Soup Kitchen board began a search for the right person.

Faye Hensley moved to Lebanon from Northern California where she received a degree in Hospitality Management at the College of the Siskiyous. Her studies included culinary arts, hotel management, meal-planning, catering and food services. Along with her education she had experience working in food banks in several cities.

A friend invited her to help in the Soup Kitchen where she quickly fit in preparing great meals. In a few weeks, her skills and personality made it apparent that she was "the answer to the organization's prayers for help," according to Hauck.

August 2001, Hensley became the first employee of the Lebanon Soup Kitchen. She worked seven hours each Monday, Wednesday and Friday, but also donated her efforts at other times. Her job description included; planning menus, organizing volunteers, cooking, cleaning, purchasing food and recording donations received.

"I'm really excited," Hensley told The Lebanon Express in an August 1, 2001 article. "It's called the Soup Kitchen, but it's definitely not just soup. That's just a title. One night we served leg of lamb. It's always different."

She thought "soup" in the title was misleading and referred to the Soup Kitchen as "Lebanon Country Club."

"Good management saves money and she was a good manager," Hauck told me one afternoon. "She was an imaginative cook and had suggestions on how to rescue stuff that may have too much salt or pepper."

"She didn't judge. She always said, "give people a chance,"" a volunteer described Faye's attitude. "She was a good worker."

Faye's work went beyond preparation and meals. She helped the youth with food drives. They combed neighborhoods to hang door knockers, a list of items the Soup Kitchen could use, on door knobs. The following week they returned to pick up whatever may be donated. The items were taken to St. Martin's Episcopal Church where adult volunteers helped sort them.

Another project that extended beyond her regular work hours was coloring eggs with her grandchildren at Easter. After the dining hall was cleaned on Good Friday, Faye, her grandchildren, and another volunteer spent the evening decorating eggs. The bright colors were a highlight for the children at Monday's dinner.

Faye worked hard. Lifting heavy boxes or pans of food began to aggravate her previously injured back. Many times she worked in pain to complete her job. Other volunteers tried to do more of the physical work for her, but the discomfort still grew to be too much. Regretfully, she resigned in 2004 and moved back to California.

An ad was placed in the local paper for the manager position. Kandi Gregory read the ad and briefly thought of applying. Kandi was a stay-at-home mom with five children. Her oldest son, 20, lived on his own but she dedicated her time to her three teenage daughters and her 9-year-old special-needs son. She had not worked outside her home in years and didn't feel qualified. But the idea of working at the Soup Kitchen kept returning to her thoughts.

"I decided to volunteer, even though the manager job had been filled." Kandi's gentle eyes glistened in her round face as she talked with me during a break. "I immediately felt like I was at home. The ladies who worked here were uplifting and encouraging. It was a warm environment. And still is," she laughed.

"This was the Lord's intervention to get me out of the house. I felt like I was in a shell at home. This was a wonderful place; the best place for me to get back into social activity. It was a big shot in the arm for me." She looked across the kitchen to several women talking. "Majel was the first person to make me feel warm, then everyone else did."

While volunteering at the Soup Kitchen, Kandi continued to look for a full-time job. She applied for a position at the Jefferson Post Office but her interview did not go well. "My confidence was low." She explained. "At the Soup Kitchen, I grew as a person and in confidence. That personal growth made the second interview (at the Post Office) go much better."

The improved interview helped her secure a part-time job at the Jefferson Post Office, with her name on a waiting list for a full-time position. The Postal delivery route she began left her with time to continue volunteering at the Soup Kitchen.

On several occasions, the new manager at the Soup Kitchen was unable to be at the kitchen on serving days. Kandi filled in for her. Those opportunities allowed Kandi to become more familiar with the operations and the people. When the manager left, Kandi felt comfortable accepting the job. Many experienced volunteers gave her helpful guidance and her easy-going attitude made the transition to manager an easy step.

"The volunteers are the best group of people and the clients are in good spirits," her soft voice proclaimed as she sipped coffee.

Their appreciation rewarded her for the willingness she gave to help anytime. One evening, John, a guest, arrived early at the back door, avoiding the guests starting to gather at the serving door. He carried a pink vase that held three silk, white roses, their pedals tipped in pink. "These are for Kandi," his raspy voice sighed. "Tell her; thanks for the bus ticket," he requested, giving the flowers to a volunteer.

The volunteer walked through the busy kitchen and handed Kandi the vase. "These are for you. John said, "Thanks for the bus ticket.""

"They are beautiful," Kandi's familiar grin raised beneath her rosy cheeks, "but he didn't have to do that." She examined the delicate flowers and sat them on the table in front of the person taking the evening count. "Let's set them here so everyone can enjoy them."

Kandi enjoyed her work as manager but with four children at home, she continued to pursue the better-paying job at the Post Office. When she was asked to work Mondays for another delivery driver, she took the opportunity to work, hoping it may lead to full-time employment.

A volunteer cook, Bruce, managed Kandi's duties on Mondays. In June 2007, when Bruce could no longer help, another cook, Janet Contreras, became the Monday supervisor.

Kandi continued to split her time between the Post Office and the Soup Kitchen while her son's deteriorating health condition also demanded more time. Twelve-year-old Devon needed a kidney transplant. Kandi's sister offered one of her kidneys and plans began for the surgery. September 2007, Devon entered Oregon Health Science University hospital in Portland for the transplant.

The surgery was completed without complications but Devon needed to remain near the doctors for observations. Kandi and her son stayed in Portland for another month.

Janet gladly filled in for Kandi to allow her the time with her son during his recovery. Kandi planned to return to work when Janet was leaving for a vacation in California. However, the Post Office increased Kandi's hours, interfering ever more with the Soup Kitchen schedule. Kandi never returned.

Janet was looking forward to Kandi's return and went to California confident that her temporary position as manager was over. Her celebration was short-lived when she received a phone call pleading for her to be the full-time manager.

Again, the Soup Kitchen Board felt that God had brought the right person to continue His work in feeding people. Janet graciously accepted the job. "I felt honored to be asked," she timidly smiled. "It is a ministry that makes my heart feel good."

Janet was born and grew up in Portland but moved to California shortly after she married in 1963. In May 2003, she moved to Lebanon to be near a son. "He moved me in on a Thursday, we had dinner for Mothers Day and he moved back to California on Monday. I knew no one here!" Janet remembers the abandonment she felt after her son's unexpected departure.

The Elks Lodge provided her a way of meeting people and staying active, but she missed the feeling of belonging she had with her friends in California. During one of her sad days in the summer of 2006, a friend invited her to cook at the Soup Kitchen. "Why not," she shrugged? "I like to play with food and I never knew how to cook for one or two. I always cooked for crowds, even at home I cooked too much." She began by cooking once a month.

"I enjoy people from the various churches who help." Janet sat wearily in a hard, metal chair as she took a break from cooking to visit with me. "Sometimes you don't know if what you do helps anyone. But here, you know you've warmed tummies."

The transition from cook to manager was a growing experience. "I had no one to train me. Kandi and Joyce (board chair) were gone. All I had were some notes. Now I have overwhelming feelings of responsibility to see that things are right." Many cooks and volunteers have helped Janet learn the details of the job. "There are some good cooks. I can leave and know that everything is done."

Everything always works out. "We may think we are going to be short on help, then volunteers start showing up. It is the same with everything. God just provides."

Janet enjoys working with the people sent to serve time for community service. She admitted they need to do the necessary work but added, "I want this to be a happy place. I want them to come back feeling good." She treated everyone; community service, volunteer or guest; with the same concern so they felt comfortable being there. Wanting others to feel good, even if for a short time, is what the Soup Kitchen is about.

She has seen the support from the generous community. "I was blown away at Christmas with the amount of money donations and food and everything that was given. It was very impressive."

Janet gives back to the community with more than her work at the Soup Kitchen. She got up at 4:30 AM one Saturday morning to cook a benefit breakfast for the Lebanon Gleaners. She helped with benefits at the Elks Lodge for their charities.

Janet would like to see a change in how people view the organization. "I would like the Soup Kitchen's reputation to be more a Community Kitchen. Of the people who come, not many are homeless. The kitchen serves the community for anyone who is hungry or needs fellowship during a meal."

Each of the managers remained strong in their leadership. Romans 15:1-2 tells us we should all be strong for those who aren't. "We who are strong ought to bear with the failings of the weak and not to please ourselves. Each of us should please his neighbor for his good, to build him up."

The time guests spend at the Soup Kitchen is only a bleep in their lives. But whether it is the food or the fellowship, they should leave happier than when they came. The managers tried to make that happen.

Sample Menu:
Scrambled Eggs
Biscuits and Gravy
Fruit
Dessert

Photo by Nancey West
Janet at Halloween

Baked in Fellowship

The table is a meeting place, a gathering ground, the source of sustenance and nourishment, festivity, safety, and satisfaction.

Laurie Colwin

Long lines formed in front of the Soup Kitchen doors at the end of each month. The lines dropped dramatically as soon as a new month began and government subsidy checks were available. The lines fluctuated, as did the people who came. That is, except for those who made the gathering for meals a part of their lives. The atmosphere of belonging brought people back three days a week all month long. Friendships formed that often took care and compassion beyond the doors.

People who came regularly often sat in the same chair each night. This was true for the group of diners sitting around the first table who had known one another for many years.

Arlene grew up in Lebanon, the daughter of a prominent mill owner. She served her country as a nurse at Emmanuel Hospital in Portland during WWII. After the war she married and raised one son while working for several local doctors and at the Lebanon Hospital, which later became the library. Before her thin fingers grew stiff with arthritis, she was a talented painter and gave many of her scenery and flower paintings away. Part of a large mural in the entry of the First Christian Church gave evidence of her talents as she worked with others to create the outdoor scenes.

She stayed involved in several organizations, though she ever had a driver's license. She relied on others to give her rides to where she needed to go. Her yard was her enjoyment, but at 85 years old and stooped with bone degeneration and a bad hip, it was difficult for her do the work needed to display the beauty it once held.

Arlene lived alone for nearly thirty years. "You don't know what it is like to stare at four walls all the time," she once told me when I gave her a ride home. She didn't have a TV or radio and could hardly hear to talk on the phone. She often felt isolated and alone. Genna or Majel would pick her up and bring to the Soup Kitchen. She enjoyed spending time with the volunteers. "I fill the sugar, salt and pepper on the tables. I'm slow but I work at it." She told me how she helped, but mostly, she liked to visit.

At the other end of the same table sat Rebecca, another guest who grew up in Lebanon. Rebecca was raised with four brothers and four sisters. "My father worked at the Santiam Mill in Sweet Home. He worked hard but there never was enough food or money. I left to get my GED in the Job Corps at Tongue Point." She explained the hardships of a large family. While in the Job Corps she attended classes in bookkeeping and later took secretarial studies at LBCC.

After graduation from LBCC, she got married and had three children, two girls and a boy. The family lived in the Albany and Lebanon area before Rebecca and her husband divorced seven years later. She worked at a cannery until her feet couldn't tolerate the long hours of standing. She had scoliosis, which are sideways curves in the spine, which made standing or walking painful. She quit her job and received disability payments.

Rebecca started coming to the Soup Kitchen about a year after it opened. Her four-year-old son, Chris, was the only child living at home and accompanied her for meals until he was in the sixth grade. The noise in the dining hall aggravated Chris' hearing problem, so he stopped coming. Rebecca continued to come without him, volunteering many times to wipe plates, clean tables and take count of the number of diners.

On Monday and Friday, Rebecca rode to the Soup Kitchen on the Dial-a-bus. Wednesday nights the bus was busy due to bingo at the Senior Center, so she walked the eight blocks. Her back condition made the walk painful but she always found a ride home. She told me about one difficulty in accepting rides. "One man offered me a ride but cigarette butts and ashes filled the ashtray and he smoked while I was in the car. I had to stop riding with him because the smoke aggravated my asthma."

Rebecca met many people coming to the Soup Kitchen, some who knew her parents. "A lady came in and asked what my maiden name was. When I told her, she said she knew me when I was 8 months old." The lady was a friend of her mother. "Another time some men came in. I didn't recognize them but later found out they were friends of my father and worked with him in the 1970s and 80s."

Rebecca saw improvement in the Soup Kitchen over the years. "They started out cooking meals with a lot of rice, macaroni and spaghetti. Then they added more meat and vegetables. Now there is more variety. There is a better selection." She commented on how behavior has also changed. "In the beginning there used to be too many drunks that cursed all the time. Now that happens only outside. The first of the month there are 3 or 4 guys who come and use the "F" word a lot." She saw different ones come and go. "There are groups of people that will come for awhile. They will leave and others will take their place."

Across the table from Rebecca, was Teresa. Her long, matted hair and thick, dark-framed glasses were a common sight at the Soup Kitchen. She began living on the street soon after high school, until HUD provided her with housing. She walked with her round, chubby face watching the ground, avoiding eye contact with others. "I am haunted by bad memories," she once told me. Her quiet demeanor left her vulnerable to be taken advantage of. And she was on many occasions.

I spent many months casually greeting Teresa before she opened up to me about the Soup Kitchen. "This is the best soup kitchen. They know how to cook good meals. It's fresh and cooked well. They have gotten better with meals." She wiped a long strand of dark hair from her face. "If I drop a tray or break a glass, they don't snap at me. When I fell, they helped me to a chair and brought my food to me. They didn't jump to conclusions and call the paramedics or police. They know my problems and how to help me; what to do or not to do and how to do it."

Her brown eyes looked toward her food or somewhere beyond me, seldom at me, as she eagerly talked. "People don't give up on me here. If I needed something, like furniture, they helped me get it." A smile raised her pink cheeks when she remembered a special friend. "Genna opens my heart up. I like hats and she buys me hats."

Next to Teresa was Jim, a friend who gave her a ride home many nights. Jim's mother, Doris, was a volunteer for many years. He came when she was there and returned after he got out of the Viet Nam war. He went to college following his service in the Army and received three degrees. He was working on his bachelors' degree when his health declined. "I have lung problems and chronic fatigue syndrome, according to the doctors." He shook his head gently. "I don't think they know." I was familiar with the condition and understood the frustration that weighed in his soft voice. The darkness below his blue eyes was evidence of his fatigue. "I live in my friend's 83-year-old grandmother's basement. It is damp in there and mold grows, so I can't clear up my lungs. So I can't work and I can't afford to move." The red in his beard was prevalent, in contrast to his brown hair.

"I eat here because I can't afford much food and it gives me a chance to get out of that moldy room." He hesitated while chewing stroganoff and noodles. "It is good for people to come here. The ones that need it aren't a problem. The problem is with the ones who won't do anything to change their lives." He tipped his head toward a couple of men leaving the dining hall. "The only trouble I've had is when someone spoke bad about Teresa." He defended his friend. "They don't need to do that."

One evening when I was eating at the "regulars'" table next to Arlene, a familiar voice interrupted. "Hi there, beautiful," Jim whispered as he set his tray on the table, his face brightened with a smile. "I knew that would get your attention," he laughed. A twinkle shone in his blue eyes, no longer underlined in dark circles. I returned a smile, glad to see him feeling well that evening. Soon after, his health improved and he returned to singing in the Community Choir, something he enjoyed and missed when he was fatigued.

At a nearby table was Marie, a small lady in her fifties. Marie first came when her brother-in-law invited her. She made friends quickly. "I like the people, both staff and others," she said one night after finishing her baked chicken. "I come here when I am sad. It gets me out of the house and also assures I get a nutritious meal at least three times a week. I try to cook meals like they do, but they're just better here." She pushed her plate away and patted her slender stomach. Her long, light-brown hair was neatly combed and held in place with a large barrette. Mahogany eyes complemented her fair complexion and pink cheeks.

"I like helping people." Marie explained why she worked at the Lord's Storehouse once a week and helped at the Soup Kitchen whenever she could. "They don't have to ask, I just do what's needed. That's the type of person I am." Marie's gentle words and soft smile brought comfort and encouragement to those she talked and joked with. Her friendliness hid her low self-esteem. "I was in special education in school and felt rejected by my sister because of it." Some nights she brought a book, usually Louis L'Amour, to quietly read.

The Soup Kitchen is truly a gathering ground that provides nourishment as well as the satisfaction and safety of being among friends. The Bible tells us in Proverbs 15:17, "It is better to have a meal of vegetables where there is love, than to have a fattened calf with hatred." Both the love and the fattened calf are served and give great satisfaction to those around the tables at the Soup Kitchen.

Sample Menu:
Hamburgers
Potato Wedges
Green Salad
Mixed Fruit
Dessert

Pans the Future

The ordinary arts we practice every day at home are of more importance to the soul than their simplicity might suggest.

Thomas Moore

Mattie squeezed her thin, six-year-old frame between a large man in a worn black jacket and the table stacked with serving trays. Her small hand reached up as her mother pulled it back. "Wait your turn," Diana ordered. The man, waiting in front of them in the Soup Kitchen line, shifted his weight away from the table as he peered down at the child pressing against his leg. With the added room, Mattie quickly darted through the opening, reached above her head and pulled a tray from the top of the pile. Inching along the table she reached toward the containers filled with silverware. A husky man glanced down and stepped forward, allowing her room to collect one spoon and one fork. She carried her supplies and stood in front of her mother. Mattie timidly looked up at her mother's disapproving glare and turned her sad face toward the floor.

The family moved slowly through the line for their portion of chicken, macaroni and cheese, salad, fruit and dessert. Mattie asked for two glasses of milk, which she typically never drank. A young volunteer carried her tray to an empty table near the back. Mattie followed, her eyes watching the tiles along the floor. As they stopped at an empty table, Blake, her ten-year-old brother, slipped past them to take the end seat. "I wanted to sit there," Mattie whined, watching her brother settle into her desired chair.

"I'll set your food at this place," the teenager said as she removed the plate and glass from the tray.

"No, I want to sit here," Mattie pushed her brother's shoulder.

"Just sit here," Diana jerked a chair away from the table.

"Noooooo." Mattie bumped her own shoulder into Blake's causing him to drop a spoonful of macaroni and cheese. "I want to sit here." Blake ignored her typical fussing.

Mattie gently leaned her back against him and stopped whining while she cautiously watched me sit in a hard, metal chair across the table. She brushed her straight, brown hair out of her face, revealing dry, discolored circles around her red eyes.

"She's not contagious, it's eczema," Diana explained as she sat down. "But the kids at school won't play with her because of it." She wiped a persistent strand of hair away from Mattie's pale cheeks. "It just won't heal. Tom started a new job but doesn't make enough to pay for medication."

Diana's thin, brown hair, cut slightly below her jaw-line, and a thin layer of bangs framed her round face, accenting her rich, chestnut eyes. She told her own story as her gaze darted around the room as if guarding who heard her.

Her raspy voice described her mother as mean and her father as absent or abusive. She never received approval from them in her childhood and never felt acceptance as a young adult when various boyfriends brought her more abusive situations. "By the time I was 18, I had more trauma than most people will ever know." She confided that her current relationship was different. "He is not like the others. He doesn't hurt me."

She hesitated while pointing to Mattie's plate. "Eat this!"

"No." Mattie whined, still standing beside her chair.

"I'm a strong person," Diana continued, while chewing. "I wasn't raised with religion but I have a spiritual connection. I have guardian angels. They protect me from everyone, including myself.

"God has always got me through." She again pointed to Mattie's plate, "Eat!" Mattie only looked away. "I don't think she feels good," Diana rationalized before continuing her own story. "I have scoliosis. The doctors say I shouldn't be walking. But I am. Sometimes, it is not easy."

Her focus moved around the room at the volunteers and guests. "God sends me people when I need them. There are good people here. I wouldn't make it through if not for here. Food stamps just don't last all month. This helps stretch my budget."

Renee, the oldest child, moved easily among the other guests and smiled at volunteers as she helped carry plates to the front. She had shoulder-length, curly brown hair and would be tall, like her mother.

Blake shared his mother's reluctance to make eye contact with anyone. His hollow, brown eyes held a pleading for approval as he glanced toward his mother.

Diana nodded toward Blake. "His teachers say he is mentally slow," she explained as he looked away. "He's 3 years behind for his age. He has asthma and eczema, not as bad as Mattie's. I don't think his teachers want to work with him."

Drinking the last of her orange juice, Diana sighed, "We don't live far from here but it is small. We may be getting a bigger house, as soon as Tom gets his fines paid off." She abruptly stopped talking, stood up and motioned toward the door. "Let's go," she told her kids.

The family gathered their coats and bag of take-home food and without acknowledging my parting words, walked away.

Diana's family, including her boyfriend, Tom, came regularly for meals. One evening, the rest of the family was eating when Blake arrived. I was taking count and talked to him while he waited in line. "I'm late because I'm working a few hours a day at the candy store. I wrecked a friend's 4-wheeler and am paying for the damage."

"I'm proud of you for taking responsibility!" I patted him on the shoulder.

An unfamiliar light glimmered in his brown eyes as a smile crept across his face. "I'd like to keep working after that's paid to buy one for myself."

"I hope you do." I told him as he picked up a tray and stepped toward the food counter.

My hopes for Blake to build some self-esteem were short-lived as I watched behaviors change in the family over the following weeks. Tom came infrequently and Diana appeared more agitated with the kids each night. One evening, Diana and Mattie arrived with matching haircuts; a Mohawk on top with long strands down their backs, streaked in red and purple.

Only a few nights later, Diana came in alone. She didn't eat. She wanted to tell Genna why she was no longer comfortable coming here. Tom was in jail and Child Services had taken the kids. She was too embarrassed to face all the people who would question her family's whereabouts. I was sad that she felt someone, a volunteer or another guest, may judge her for her situation. We wanted to be there for emotional support but Diana never returned.

Not all children who came to the Soup Kitchen were beaten down by the poor choices of their parents. Some found the experience expanded their views. Randy and Brenda brought their children when they were pre-school age. The family came to the Soup Kitchen shortly after it opened, with encouragement from Randy's brother. "Our kids grew up coming here," Brenda told me as she waited for Randy to finish his meal one evening.

Randy and Brenda lived on a farm and their son and daughter had little social life. Interactions at the Soup Kitchen were good for them, Brenda explained, "It helped with their social manners. It helped develop skills and respect for parents and for others. Sometimes as a parent, I would be stressed. Zee would talk nicely with the kids and they learned manners. Kids should be respectful to those helping them. They should say "please" and "thank you" and clean up after themselves. Volunteers should say something to kids when they are out of line, if it is done nicely. My kids tended to be spoiled. The experience here helped to restore boundaries. It taught them to appreciate a variety of foods. The food here may not be like what I cooked at home. They learned to like different things." Randy nodded in agreement while he finished a piece of cherry pie.

Brenda handed her plate to a volunteer and continued. "The Soup Kitchen is the best thing that happened to Lebanon. Lebanon couldn't exist without it. It's good to socialize and made holidays special."

Both Randy and Brenda have volunteered their help at times. "It is a friendly staff," Randy added, pushing his empty plate to the center of the table. "They helped me find boots for work. Coming here has kept our family fed when we couldn't." The couple returned for meals when needed. "We use it to play catch-up with the bills."

Like Randy and Brenda, other families came who had solid family values but needed assistance to make ends meet. An unemployed musician would bring his wife and 11 children. They lived in an old trailer and traveled around the country looking for gigs. "All the kids were very well-behaved," a volunteer smiled as she talked of the cleanly dressed children, one who was a dwarf. Another couple, who lived in a one room studio apartment, brought their seven children. All were well-mannered.

A family came from Albany with their eight children. The parents and children would each go back through the line for seconds and thirds to fill containers they brought with them. The manager explained they were welcome to eat what they could while here but were not to fill their own containers. Take-outs were given at the end of the meal, if food was left over. The family was asked to wait until the serving ended to ask for something to take home. The family stopped coming.

Children sometimes came with their mother, fleeing abusive situations. One woman asked for sleeping bags so the family could sleep in the park. Another, with two toddlers, needed a place to sleep for one night. She was given a voucher for a room at one of the local motels. Before she left, shoes and clothes were gathered for the children and lunches were made for them to have the next day.

Many children came alone. They may not have anyone at home to cook a meal for them. One twelve year old came regularly, bringing friends or an uncle when they would join him.

Another boy, about the same age, lived only a few houses away. Joey wondered what church had the bells that woke him up. When he met the interim pastor, Peter Webster, he was eager to accept his invitation to church. One Sunday, Joey arrived at church for Sunday school, stayed through church and mingled during coffee hour, devouring as many cookies as possible. He learned about the Soup Kitchen and began coming every serving night.

His bright red hair and smiling face full of freckles was seen often at youth activities at the church and helping clean plates at the Soup Kitchen. I grew fond of him and his sometimes over-eagerness to be help. He once told me, "I don't have to come here. I just want to help out and have a delectable meal." He emphasized "delectable. "Sometimes I have to cook at home and I don't want to, so I come here."

Joey stopped coming when his family moved across town and the Soup Kitchen wasn't so convenient. I often wondered what happened to him when he showed up for a meal one night. I was eager to talk with him and learn how he was doing. He told me that he just received a Social Security check indicating that his father died. "We kept in contact awhile but I haven't talk to him in six months. This is how I found out he must have died. I don't when, or how." Sadness edged into his usually cheery voice.

I asked if he was coming back regularly again. Excitement returned to his words. "I'm going with my step-dad to Colorado. He has a job there. We can work together and get enough money to buy a house." He left again but this time I sent my best wishes and prayers with him.

One boy had no one at home during the day. He came to the Soup Kitchen but it wasn't opened. Joyce told me of finding him sitting outside because he had no place to stay. She gathered some veggie rolls and biscuits for him to eat. Later that afternoon, she found him still sitting there. "Do you feel better?" she asked. His eyes lit and he beamed, "Oh, yes."

The Soup Kitchen works to be a positive influence in everyone's lives, especially the children. Volunteers face the challenge of correcting a child, whether it is for manners, language or behavior, without interfering with the parent's role. The rules are clear on what language and behavior is permitted.

Manners are a matter of courtesy. If a child learns those at home, we could reinforce them at the Soup Kitchen with a gentle reminder. But when manners and courtesy are foreign, it is not our job to teach them, except by our actions.

Proverbs 22:6 tells us to "train a child in the way he should go, and when he is old he will not turn from it." For those children who aren't taught courtesy or respect at home, we hope to show a glimpse of it. It is our hope that they take that simple kindness into the world with them.

Sample Menu:
Chicken A-La-King
Noodles
Corn
Cabbage Slaw
Bread
Watermelon
Dessert

Raises Hope

It is never too late to be what you might have been.

George Elliot

Life seldom turns out the way one planned as a young person. Often people find themselves in living conditions they never imagined. The situation becomes a way of life for many people, to others it is a stage they are passing through. The Soup Kitchen can be a stepping stone for those who work to improve their surroundings.

One who worked hard to pull her life together was Stacy. She came one night in desperation, after her boyfriend, who she shared a house with, kicked her out. She had two small children and her ailing father to care for with no job and no place to live. A camper on her pickup provided shelter as long as she found a place to park. But this night they all needed a warm meal and the baby needed diapers. Those needs were readily met and clothing for the children would be available, if she returned during the next meal. One volunteer spent the following day shopping for clothes for the baby girl and jeans for the four-year-old boy.

"Thank you so much," Stacy's soft voice purred as she looked over the clothes. Her blue eyes glistened as she held a spring dress up to the tiny girl.

During each meal, Stacy told where she was parking the camper that week and how hard she was looking for a job. I enjoyed her polite, easy manner as we visited. She worried about her son's activity disturbing others in the dining room though the boy was well-mannered and a joy to be with.

After I showed him the many books and puzzles in the Book Nook, an area at the back of the room, he spent as much time there as he did eating.

When Stacy wasn't feeding the kids or herself, she encouraged her father to eat. He often picked at his food, distracted by the severe pain in his arthritic leg.

After only a month, the family stopped coming. I missed her sweet spirit, the baby's wide smile and her son's shining eyes. Often people stopped coming and we usually never heard how they were doing but I soon learned Stacy was working at a local coffee shop. The meager salary she earned barely afforded a small apartment for the four of them. Stacy's optimistic smile assured me they would be fine.

I stopped by the coffee shop now and then to see her bright, smiling face and ask how they were doing. Her concerns were for her father. The pain in his leg was unbearable and he needed to have it amputated.

The surgery was a success and soon afterward Stacy's father returned to the Soup Kitchen. A wheelchair was available to enable him to join his family for meals. He proudly held the tiny girl on his lap as Stacy pushed him to a table. Pain once drained the color from his face but the dark tan had returned as did the shine in his aging eyes.

The food and diapers given Stacy at the Soup Kitchen were only a small step in her climb to improve her life but it was a step she appreciated.

Like Stacy, Randy appreciated help. Randy first came to the Soup Kitchen in filthy, torn clothes clinging to a skinny body in need of hygiene care. "I want to better myself," he told volunteers. He had been a carpenter before he was injured and was seeking a disability settlement. During his wait for the settlement he made several errors in judgment that left him in this sorry state.

Genna gave him clean clothes from her husband's closet and found someone to work on his pickup that just broke down. Randy bathed and got a haircut and was hardly recognizable in his new shirts and pants. When his pickup was repaired, he came to the Soup Kitchen often to help with cleanup. In gratitude for the help, he looked for ways to do more. He took a food safety course at the Elks Lodge and was proud to have his food handler's license, allowing him to help in preparation and serving of the meals.

Randy finally received money from his disability settlement. He used the money to purchase a more reliable vehicle and to rent a duplex apartment in Lebanon, near a brother and sister. Staying close to family was a common reason for people to come or return to this area.

Bud was born and raised in Lebanon and after years of living in Portland, returned to be near his mother. "I planned on drinking when I came here. I drank up there, but I was starving. I couldn't afford food so in order to eat I would sell beer that people gave me." The corners of his mouth pulled down in a frown and he shook his head as if disgusted with his own actions.

"I came here expecting a similar facility as the one I went to in Portland. The Soup Kitchen there had drunks and people selling drugs. Here the people give me hope, love and something to look forward to. They are never disapproving. They are full of life and a lot of energy. They are Christians." His large brown eyes peered from behind think, dark-rimmed glasses. "When I came here, I didn't drink. The people here helped me find work and pointed me in the right direction. They are my family." But, he didn't forget his own family. "Now I spend every Sunday morning with my mom. We go to breakfast and in the afternoon I do yard-work or something. We stick together."

Another family who moved to Lebanon to be near family was Kelly's. He, his wife and their high school aged daughter needed help from her parents when Kelly lost his job in Washington. He came to the Soup Kitchen alone, looking for employment opportunities as much as a warm meal. The dingy denim jeans, cut off at the top of his heavy work boots were evidence of the grey-haired man's occupation. "I'm Kelly," he extended a tanned and weathered hand as I sat across the table from him one night. He rolled the sleeves of his black and grey hickory shirt before he began to eat. "I've been here 3 months and have called every logging company in the phone book. Most say to just keep checking back."

I knew many logging companies in the area, but none that were hiring. "What experience do you have?" I asked, thinking I could pass the information on.

"I have done every job in the woods, except shovel operator. The shovel is what loads the trucks," he began to explain but I said I knew what it was. His husky voice continued with pride and frustration, "They log differently here than where I came from. I am a good worker but there just isn't anything available here." He stirred melted cheese into his home-made chili. "I've been logging for 22 years and have never been hurt in the woods. That is an accomplishment," he explained proudly. I knew it was.

"Maybe I could call some friends in Sweet Home," I offered.

"I called some there," he interrupted. "They wanted me to drive to Sweet Home."

"You can't do that?" I tried to keep the surprise out of my voice.

"I don't have a driver's license. But I'm going to get one as soon as I can."

My heart sank. Without a driver's license he couldn't get to a job. "It seems that would be the priority."

"I have to have $450 for rent by the 10th. I can't afford a car right now."

There was the familiar cycle of many who I meet here. No job, no money. No money, no home or car or whatever it would take to get a job. I could do nothing to break his circle. I would ask my logging friends, but I didn't know any that could provide a ride from Lebanon to the worksite.

When Kelly returned a few nights later, I gave him several phone numbers for possible leads on jobs. He came back each week with the same dead-end results. Then he stopped coming and I hoped that meant he found a job.

Sometimes we never know when someone makes the right connection to turn their life around. Sometimes we do. One homeless man returned to the Soup Kitchen to thank the volunteers for the support they gave him. Their kindness was part of how he began succeeding in small things and built a better life.

"The plans of the diligent lead to profit as surely as haste leads to poverty," Proverbs 21:5 confirms that success in life takes effort. Stories like the ones here are an encouragement. The work of the Soup Kitchen can be a positive influence to the ones who are willing to make the little extra help a step toward their dream.

Sample Menu:
Chicken Salad
Carrots
Beets
Green Salad
Applesauce
Dessert

Seared By Life

The body must be nourished, physically, emotionally and
spiritually.
We're spiritually starved in this culture—not underfed but
undernourished.

Carol Hornig

The dining room was busy with people carrying trays loaded with
their evening meals. I watched the activity, recognizing many faces
from years of regular attendance. Other faces, I did not recognize.

One man, probably in his 60s, faced me from the next table. His neatly
trimmed sideburns and goatee were streaked with grey in contrast to his wavy
black hair. The tanned, rough skin of his round face was salted with day-old
stubble. Bushy eyebrows shadowed his dark, deep set eyes. I watched as he
quietly ate taco casserole and green beans. The crevasses snaking away from
the corner of his mouth and eyes deepened when he smiled and gave a slight
tip of his head in acknowledgment to another man joining him at that table.

The second man was younger, though not by much. His long, narrow
face continued the characteristics of his tall, thin body. A hint of grey showed
in his well manicured mustache and sideburns. Dark, sandy hair hung inches
below a wide-brimmed straw hat with a white tassel dangling from the back.
He returned a nod to the first man as he slowly lowered his cartoon-like
figure onto the metal chair. His lower jaw continually moved up and down
but no sound escaped his narrow mouth. His hand was slow but steady as he
lifted his fork to eat.

I knew nothing of either man except what I saw before me. Who they
are now and who they were in the past may be quite different. Circumstances

or bad choices, or both, can lead someone to need or crave company from others in similar stages of their lives. But they are here now. That is all I need to know, or I become like those James scolded in James 2:1-5; "…don't show favoritism. Suppose a man comes into your meeting wearing a gold ring and fine clothes, and a poor man in shabby clothes also comes in. If you show special attention to the man wearing fine clothes and say, "Here's a good seat for you," but say to the poor man, "you stand there" or "sit on the floor by my feet," have you not discriminated among yourselves and become judges with evil thought?"

Looking at outward appearances tempts us to judge, but knowing details about someone often gives us more ways to judge. Preconceived ideas about these people and why they come can only breed the judgment Jesus warned us not to have for one another. The only way to keep those thoughts from us is to see others with the compassion that God sees them.

My thoughts were interrupted as I felt a light tap on my shoulder. I looked up into Genna's concerned face. She tipped her head slightly gesturing to look behind me. She whispered, "You're in Ray's chair."

I turned to my left to find a tall, elderly gentlemen patiently waiting near the end of the table. "I'm sorry," I apologized and moved to the next chair. Genna tapped me again. "That's his wife's chair."

People are creatures of habit and a few guests are not comfortable unless sitting in their usual chair. Ray claimed the two chairs at the end of the first table for his wife, Elma, and him. In fact, he wouldn't eat until he was able to sit in his chair. I looked around for his frail wife. "Is your wife here tonight?"

"Not tonight. She wasn't feeling well," he explained in a deep voice that sounded as if it were filtered through marbles.

With his wife absent, I asked if I could join him. Soon the husky man was telling me his story.

"I grew up on a dairy, getting up at 4 a.m. to milk. I worked all summer, with 30 days on and four days off." He seemed eager to tell me of his hard-working life. His front teeth were missing but the others were worn on one side leaving them sharp and allowing him to easily eat his ham and potatoes. His long nose tipped inward at the end, resembling a hook. Thick, red spots covered his hairless head and his rosy face was speckled with white stubs.

"I used to farm. Grew corn and beans. I had farms scattered from Coburg to Corvallis." He swallowed and added, "I had 400 employees."

While continuing to eat, he mumbled as though talking to himself. "I married my first wife in 1964. She helped me with the farm but then she left." He took a deep breath as a hint of anger edged into his voice. "We had three boys. One works for the CIA." Pride filled his crystal blue eyes as he looked at me and nodded his head to assure me it was true.

"I farmed until the 1980s when I was in a bus wreck. I moved to the trailer park but had to have a nurse care for me. She's now my wife."

As Ray talked, he often repeated parts of his stories, sometimes contradicting himself. "I still have 200 acres," he explained.

His movements were slow and rigid from his eighty-plus years and injuries from the bus wreck he referred to several times. "You must have someone to help you farm that many acres," I concluded.

"No," he rapidly shot back. "I do all the work myself." He again described his farming empire and the bus wreck that crippled him. I let him continue as if it were the first time I heard the story. Ray was proud of the life he lived, at least how he remembered he lived. I let him brag of his accomplishments and the prestige he may have had.

Ray found comfort living in the past, but others needed to make amends with it, such as Ted. Ted was a short, heavy-set man in his fifties who pushed a wheelchair containing all his belongings, including a cane hanging from its back. He moved cautiously with each step while a young volunteer followed with his tray. His receding hairline enlarged his round face and his reddened eyes were underlined with dark bags. I visited with this man earlier in the week during his first meal here. He told me he lived in Lebanon years ago but left his wife to go to Reno. Now he was trying to find her. He wheezed as he explained, "I am dying of cancer and we need to settle our affairs."

Ted's failing health brought him here in search of mending a part of his broken past. Likewise, Paul had a devastating health issue in his past that led him to be a long-time guest. I glanced around the room to find him. Paul, a short, skinny man in his fifties, always waited until the last person in line had his tray before he got his food. There were still people waiting in line, so I turned toward the hallway. Sure enough, he was sitting on a bench, talking. No one was around but that didn't interrupt his conversation. Deep crow's-foot lines trace his dark, tanned face as he occasionally smiled and laughed out loud. His grey-streaked hair was pulled back tightly in a ponytail that hung in long ringlets down his back. His bushy beard and mustache were nearly white.

I was told Paul's story. He was married once. He worked in construction when one afternoon a large beam from a partially completed roof fell and struck him in the head. Paul had serious brain damage. He survived but could not return to the life he knew. He was living alone in a small apartment and had a bicycle for transportation. His clothes were generally dirty and torn. If he wasn't wearing shorts, he would only wear Levis 501. Genna bought him a pair of the jeans on EBay but he remained in his torn ones. Genna asked each night why he didn't wear the new ones. He had no particular reason. Eventually, he showed up wearing the new, clean pair.

I said "hello," as Paul walked near me to peek around the corner and see if anyone was waiting at the food counter. There was no line. He turned to talk to me but his words came so fast I wasn't sure what he said. He ended with a laugh. I smiled, not knowing what the joke was.

I'm not as comfortable around Paul as I once was. One night I was taking count when he came in. His forehead was furrowed with deep lines and his eyes were glassy and narrowed in an eerie glare. From the words I could understand I thought he was upset about something not being fair or right. I acknowledged him only with a slight nod. He continued his raving as he picked up his tray and silverware, glancing toward me often. I was thankful when he turned his back to me to receive his food but he suddenly whirled around and stared directly at me with cold, steely eyes. "And I didn't do it!" He raised his voice louder than I had ever heard him. Just as quickly, he returned to get his food. As he walked past me with his tray, he didn't say a word but watched me with narrowed eyes. Minutes later, my heart rate returned to normal. I explained the situation to another volunteer. She responded, "He can be very dangerous, I'm told."

Tonight, Paul was quiet.

My attention turned to Vern, another man with declining health. Vern is in his mid-sixties, of medium height, with sparse brown hair. He is slender, except for his protruding mid-section. He always dresses in clean, fresh khaki pants and a nice sweeter. At one time he was probably a dashing man. Vern was a retired veteran with cancer. His back was slightly bent and he shuffled along with the aid of a cane, reminding me of Tim Conway's character on "The Carol Burnett Show." I tried talking with him once but his weak voice left his words indistinguishable. A faint smile showed spaces for several missing teeth. But it was his eyes that deeply touched me. They were a rich brown, gentle but sad. Not a sadness of self-pity but a longing to communicate; a loneliness from not feeling acknowledged and accepted.

Acceptance was really what we all looked for. People came here for food but they reacted to the way they were treated. It reminded me of a volunteer's comment years ago when we were starting the Soup Kitchen. She said, "The Soup Kitchen is more important than filling empty stomachs. It may be the only smile someone gets that day. God means for us to help them and show them respect."

Respect was shown in the eagerness of the volunteers to help a young family with two children get their food and settle at a table. I had never seen the family before. The mother's stringy, unkempt straw-colored hair hung over her thin face, surrounding the wire-rimmed glasses loosely perched on her pointy nose. Her paste-colored skin looked like it was hung on bones. She was medium height, slightly shorter than the rugged man beside her. His shaven head was covered with a red bandana and earrings dangled from each ear. Blue eyes bulged from his ruddy, round face. His faded blue jeans were cut below the knees, leaving short strings dangling. A girl, maybe three- or four-years old, was timidly standing beside the woman. Dark, precious eyes peered from behind her long, brown hair that desperately needed introduction to a brush. The child's complexion was soft and smooth. The man pushed a stroller; an older one with a seat in a wire frame, not one with places to hold diaper bags, purses or drinks. A bright blanket covered the quiet bundle inside.

My heart ached for the desperation, or embarrassment, that engulfed the young mother's eyes. The father humbly thanked the volunteers for their help. I didn't know their story. I did know they, and every other Soup Kitchen guest, deserved our help, our encouragement and our respect to nurture them physically, emotionally and spiritually.

Sample Menu:
Hot Cakes
Eggs
Sausage
Green Salad
Applesauce
Dessert

Fold In Gently

"The worst sin towards our fellow creatures is not to hate them, but to be indifferent to them; that's the essence of inhumanity."

George Bernard Shaw

Being a good neighbor was one of the Soup Kitchen's priorities. A few local people expressed concern with the poor and homeless gathering in one location for a meal, suspecting vandalism and violence to increase. Volunteers tried to watch for behaviors and situations that could lead to problems.

An unlit area behind the church became one of our first concerns. Large lilac bushes gave cover for suspected drug dealing and supplying beer for minors. The church property sat behind a convenience store and gas station, providing easy access to beer. In one area people built small fires, which attracted more people. Farther down the back of the church another area was used for a bathroom. Fights would occasionally break out. One night there was a knife fight, luckily with no injuries.

The Soup Kitchen volunteers didn't always know when they were a good influence for change. Two brothers, Bob and James, were participants in the campfires behind the building, littering and bringing alcohol onto church property. Volunteers and police talked to them many times about their activities. They slept in the park and hung out with others in similar lifestyles. Offering healthy meals was the only help the volunteers thought they gave. The brothers moved to Portland and returned several years later to visit the Soup Kitchen. Both brothers left their addictive habits and started living successful lives. James was quite creative as a poet. He shared his handwritten poems and stories at the Soup Kitchen. Zee, co-coordinator, gave him a used word processor to encourage his writing. She cherishes the stories he gave her.

Police patrols were a deterrent but other measures were needed to curtail the problem. Bob Hauck and others from the church cut out the bushes that provided cover and built a fence from the edge of the church to the back fence of the gas station. The fence eliminated trespassing onto neighbor's property. The open area at the end of the church could be more clearly monitored, reducing harmful activity.

The problems decreased but did not disappear. One night two men in front of the Soup Kitchen started fighting about a bicycle. A volunteer thought he had settled the disagreement when the two began shoving each other to be first in line. One of the men huffed off to his car and brought back a baseball bat. He started to swing at the other man but ended up beating a volunteer's car that was parked near the door, leaving it with several dents.

The police were called when problems appeared to be developing. If arguing began inside, the participants were asked to leave. Once outside the police could deal with them. But the dining hall remained a safe place for guests. The police were not allowed to look for or arrest diners inside the building.

Disturbances were generally little more than yelling matches and swearing. Those people were asked to stop or leave, in respect for others. The Soup Kitchen would not tolerate those behaviors and guests respected that. Most people came wanting a peaceful place to eat. Many of the diners know each other beyond the Soup Kitchen and got along well.

"They want attention and are lonely." Genna described some of the guests. "Here they feel love; there's no backstabbing. But they have to get to know you before they will trust you."

People came back because they trusted and knew that they could get more than food. The Soup Kitchen gave a lot of bikes and tents. Sometimes the same people asked for replacements more than once. The homeless often told of getting their stuff stolen. Volunteers wanted to meet any need they could, but monitoring was established to prevent taking items just to sell or trade.

Some people told of plans on how they were going to improve their lives. At 11 a.m. one day, a man showed up at the Soup Kitchen door, his sunken eyes filled with moisture. "I haven't eaten in three days," he explained to the cooks just beginning to prepare the evening meal. "I am going to start at Teen Challenge this week, but I need food now." A strand of short, blond hair tumbled across his forehead. "I have been sober for 48 hours," he stated as if it were proof of his impending change. "I have a girlfriend who was too embarrassed to come with me," he hinted at receiving food for her also.

Janet, a cook, made sandwiches and gave him a 6-pack of fruit drink. "Come back tonight for a full meal."

"We will," he promised.

That evening, both he and his girlfriend came. "I'm glad to see you made it," Janet smiled as she dished them some Chow Mein and noodles. "Are you still going to go to Teen Challenge?" She questioned his intent.

"I'm thinking about going sometime." He shrugged as he walked away with his tray.

The initial line of guests filed through then the servers had a few minutes of quiet. Janet stepped out of the kitchen near the front door as the young man and his girlfriend were leaving with several men. "Thank you for the food," he smiled, walking toward the exit.

"You're welcome. I hope you are still going to start at Teen Challenge," she encouraged.

"I'm thinking about it," he said over his shoulder as he left. He never returned.

Unlike this man, Shaun did not make any promise about his future. "My motto is 'I'm living life on the installment plan.'" He laughed as I sat to talk with him one night. His smile revealed straight, white teeth. His dishwater-blond hair and deep blue eyes made him look younger than his 35-years.

"Life on the installment plan?" I questioned, knowing he was eager to tell his philosophy.

"I have been in and out of jail since I was 11 years old and placed in juvenile. I live between the times I am inside. I got out on Monday, serving two weeks for drinking." He shoveled a fork-full of salad into his mouth. "Alcohol's still a problem. I have to start in a program now."

"Are you going to stay out of jail this time?" I asked.

"I don't know," he laughed as though it wasn't important to him. His reply told me the answer.

"I'm homeless now because my roommate moved part of my stuff to the carport while I was in jail. Some things are still inside but a note on the door says I can't live there." Anger crept into his voice as his forehead furrowed.

"I was working a job steam-cleaning exhaust systems above stoves in commercial buildings. I traveled around the Northwest and California." He set his fork down and leaned back in his chair and explained, "I'll get my job back when there's an opening and I'm through treatment."

Shaun lived near the park in a tent next to his mom and step-father's tent. One night he came in with dark circles under his eyes. He stared at the food as it was added to his plate. Pinched lips took the place of his usual large smile. "You look tired tonight," I observed as I handed him a piece of cherry pie.

"Ya, I was up all night. My parents are gone and I have to watch their stuff." He yawned and blinked his red eyes. "I heard noises outside, so had to stay up to keep someone from stealing Mom's or my things."

"I hope you get more sleep tonight," I said, watching his shoulders sway from one side to the other as he walked away. His long strides carried his tall frame quickly, even when he wasn't in a hurry.

One evening following an early snow, I asked Shaun if he found shelter other than his tent. He told me he had moved in with his mom and step-father in their studio apartment. That didn't work out nearly as well as living next to each other in tents. He reported of the stress at home each time he came in.

Christmas Eve he came in late. The meal had been served and guests were choosing gifts from the tables lined with stuffed animals, toys, clothes and especially socks, the most sought after item. Shaun sat near the back of the dining room. His eyes were red, but not from fatigue. "What's going on?" I quietly asked as I brought him a plate of food.

"My mom kicked me out!" Pain rang through each word. "It's Christmas and I have to walk the streets all night because I have nowhere to go. I don't have a way to get to Albany to see if they have any beds left," he huffed, referring to the shelter 15-miles away.

I didn't know what to say. The situation was sad but without a shelter in Lebanon, I had no solution. "I'll talk to someone. Just enjoy your meal right now and we'll see what we can do."

Before long we found someone from Albany who agreed to give him a ride to Helping Hands, a homeless shelter.

That was the last time I saw Shaun. His mother came in one night, her eyes moist with tears. Her quiet voice rose with emotion, "I don't know where Shaun is. I heard he tried to kill himself. They took him to the hospital," she gulped some air and pointed the direction of the hospital. "We went out there but no one would let me see him. They took him somewhere. I don't know where." My heart ached as I pictured how I would feel if I didn't know the whereabouts of my own son. "I don't know where he is," she repeated each word slow and firm, accenting her frustration and concern. Weeks later I learned he contacted her and they again talked regularly.

I heard how Shaun was doing. But the fate of some we will never know. Others have settled into a life-long rut. Ed was 65-years-old and lived with his mother in a small cabin. She worked two jobs while he remained addicted to gambling, smoking, drinking and drugs. He had poor social skills and seldom left their home.

Sometimes the people who come here improve their lives only for a short time. One middle-aged man came regularly and befriended Joe, a volunteer. When the man became ill he struggled to walk to the Soup Kitchen and find Joe. Joe immediately took him to the hospital where he had emergency surgery to remove fluid from his brain. The near-death experience left the man with a desire to live a better life. When he recovered, he found a job. Once he began making money he returned to buying drugs until he lost his job and returned to his destructive lifestyle.

One woman asked for help and did not take it when offered. She came in with a badly abscessed tooth. Volunteers told her they would arrange for help if she would return at a designated time. The 23-year-old never returned.

Telling these stories reminds me of the angry voice on the phone when we first opened the Soup Kitchen, "You are fools for doing this. People will just take advantage of you." Were these people taking advantage of us or were they taking advantage of an opportunity that God provided them? We are only fools if we expected every diner to leave here and live their lives in accordance with our expectations. They do not come for our guidance or counsel but for compassion and acceptance.

When I first read Ephesians 4:31 "Get rid of all bitterness, rage and anger, brawling and slander along with every form of malice," I thought of the pain and brokenness brought here by people who knew all of these maladies. Then I realized it referred to all of us, volunteer or guest, when I read verse 32, "Be kind and compassionate to one another, forgiving each other, just as in Christ, God forgave you." God is telling us to look at everyone with the eyes in which we want God to see us.

Bitterness, anger and slander do not exclude the volunteers. Their whispered comments about a large person's size when he returns for a third helping holds the same malice as hateful words shouted across the dining room. Questioning someone's choice to spend money at Dutch Brothers, then to come for food is judgmental. Sarcastic tones are a form of degrading another person. All of us are to look at one another with kindness and compassion, giving each other the respect every human deserves, according to God's word.

Sample Menu:
Stroganoff
Noodles
Zucchini with tomatoes
Green Salad
Peaches
Banana Pudding

A Degree Above

When the heart has will, the hands can soon find means to
execute a good action.

Susanna Haswell Rowson

Poinsettias and tapered candles brightened the long tables covered
with green or red linens. Fine china, glasses, silverware and carefully
folded cloth napkins placed in the center of the plate decorated each
place setting. Festive Christmas music sprang from the piano at the far
end of the room near an ornament-covered tree. Heat radiated from the
gas fireplace to warm the dining hall lit with seasonal adornment.

"Your choice for the main course tonight is prime rib or baked ham," the
server explained as each guest was escorted to a table. "It is served with twice
baked potatoes and matchstick carrots with sauce or green bean almandine.
Chocolate cake or apple pie is for dessert." The server filled the stemmed
water glasses while the patrons absorbed the unusual setting.

The Soup Kitchen had been transformed into a fine restaurant for elegant
dining complete with waiters and a maitre d'. Guests wore their normal attire
of jeans, sweatshirts and heavy coats but were treated as those accustomed to
formal dress.

"Would you care for sparkling cider?" A volunteered offered a middle-
aged man. The amber drink flowed gently into the wine glass, its bubbles
sparkling as they rose to the top.

The waiter wrote each request and delivered the order to the kitchen
window.

Juices ran from the pink center of prime rib as a thick piece was cut off
and placed on a plate. A small container of au jus nestled next to it with a

73

potato along side. Long thin carrots in a thick, creamy sauce were added to complete an appetizing picture. Each plate was carefully arranged with the delectable entrees as ordered by individuals.

The season's cheer infiltrated the dining area as 100 guests, many extended families, enjoyed the special treatment. For one hour on Christmas Day, the hungry were waited on and served an elegant meal like most had never seen. This was a gift from Frank Crowley, a robust man with a giving heart.

Frank spent hours painstakingly collecting donations and preparing the meal. His hearty laughter rang through the festive atmosphere as he visited with people while his creations were being served. At the end of the meal, the poinsettias, which had been donated by a local bank, were given to guests to take home, adding more Christmas cheer to their day.

Frank once worked as director of Food Services for San Diego State University where 20,000 meals were served daily. He used that expertise to gather support for his dream of a special Christmas meal, which included dishes like Cornish game hen and shrimp cocktail, besides ham or turkey. He prepared all the dishes from scratch, including the sauces and gravies. The desserts were gifts of Roth's bakery.

The cost of a normal meal served at the Soup Kitchen was 70-90 cents. Frank would not scrimp on any of his dishes and the cost could run $3.50 a meal. He canvassed the town for donations from businesses and organizations. "I just basically go around and beg," he was quoted in a December 2001 article in the Lebanon Express. He found more than enough support to create his special meal each year without using any of the Soup Kitchen's budget. Friends and volunteers were readily available to help. They gathered in three shifts. The first came in at noon to help Frank with preparations, the second served the meal at 5 pm and the last came in to cleanup.

Frank ran a business, Computer Classroom, on Main St. in Lebanon, a few blocks from the Soup Kitchen. He closed the store on Mondays to allow himself time to cook the evening meal. After a couple of years of volunteering, he noticed that holidays did not always fall on scheduled Soup Kitchen days. Though he cooked every meal as if he were a chef in a fine diner, he wanted something special for Christmas. His brown eyes shone with pride when he worked on his unforgettable project.

Frank and his wife, Katherine, were familiar with hard times. In 1992, they were awakened in the middle of the night by a thunderous explosion, as part of the roof of their home crashed to the floor in flames. Frank, recovering from an injured knee, struggled to get Katherine's mother out of the rapidly burning house. She was recovering from a stroke and her crippled body could do little to help him. They all survived with only their bathrobes. The house and all of their belongings were a total loss.

They stayed in a local motel while considering their options. Many people brought clothes as the news of their misfortune spread. Within a few days, their insurance gave them $500 to purchase clothes and immediate essentials. Katherine and her mother went shopping in Eugene to rebuild their wardrobes. While in one store the $500 was stolen from Katherine's purse.

Friends pulled together for the couple and held a spaghetti dinner fundraiser. A band donated their time and businesses gave door prizes. Thousands of dollars were raised to help Frank and Katherine begin again. They were overwhelmed by the generosity of friends and strangers. Frank wondered how to repay all the kindness.

"Why don't you volunteer at the Soup Kitchen?" suggested one of his students at his Computer Classroom.

The idea stuck, and the large man with an equally large heart began giving back to the community even more of the compassion and generosity that had been given him. "The reward for me is not just feeding the people, though. It's being around these people who work at the Soup Kitchen. They're just great." Frank was quoted in an article in the Lebanon Express in December 2001, nearly a decade after he began cooking. "Love your neighbor as yourself," (James 2:8) was just a part of who Frank was.

Frank loved serving at the Soup Kitchen but the narrow isles of the small cooking area caused many restrictions. He had a dream of expanding the kitchen with a 20- by 30-foot addition. He pursued the idea in 1999 by soliciting materials and services, but the funds were not available for his hopes to move forward.

Frank passed away in 2002. That year, Jack and Janine LaFranchise served a special Christmas dinner in his memory. It was the last year of the elegant dining.

Frank still gave, even after his death, when a bike he donated was raffled in 2004. The proceeds went to the Soup Kitchen.

He is greatly missed, though some say he is not gone. One of the volunteers, who came after he passed away talked of a "presence" she could feel in the kitchen. When she learned about Frank, she was convinced he occasionally visits the kitchen where his heart and hands contributed so much good.

Sample Menu:
Prime Rib
Twice Baked Potato
Matchstick Carrots
Chocolate Cake
Sparkling cider

Waves of Aroma

The glow of one warm thought is to me worth more than money.

Thomas Jefferson

Mitch leaned back in the metal chair after finishing his meal. "This is not a little thing," he raised his soft voice and motioned around the nearly packed dining room. "There is more good that comes from this place than just what you do here."

His years of poverty provided experience in the street life. "People from the street have no place clean to go. This is a clean place. They come here and see people who care. Without it, people would crash and burn. People come here and see the cleaner side of life, without it being pushed at them. It's just there." His sun-baked skin and a hint of gray along his temples added to his rugged good-looks. "Other places don't have this. The best gift is the gift of giving. The people here have that."

Mitch smiled and continued. "Good will changes people. It shines a little light into lives. A lot of people don't have a light at all, but this is a bright light to them, like life-giving oxygen. It renews a belief in life." His dark hand slid his plate to the side and he leaned on the table. His rich, brown eyes stared at me as if to emphasize his point. "Outside may be hate but it doesn't come in here. People become more than friends. More like a family. It is deep seated."

He drank the last of his milk and set it in the empty plate. "The food here is good, better than some restaurants."

Mitch served 20 years in the Army and continued serving in the National Guard while working as a pipe fitter. He moved his wife and three daughters to the Lebanon area from Los Angeles after a bullet come through a window in their home. He shook his head. "L.A. is no place to raise a kid."

When the girls were grown, Mitch's wife left him, taking their small son. She severed connections with Mitch and denied him access to his youngest child. He took medication prescribed for the depression and anxiety that developed after the separation. It made him itch all over. His self-esteem was undermined and he lost his job.

"I saw a number of counselors and psychiatrists but none were compassionate. They didn't care about me as a person." Bitterness slowly crept into his voice. He hesitated. "They could learn from the people here." He motioned to a volunteer clearing plates from another table.

Marie sat in the metal chair next to Mitch and nodded in agreement as he talked. They had been together since 1994. Marie had two sons who live in Reno and a third who worked at a small mill in Scio and lived in a tent next to the one she and Mitch shared.

Mitch and Marie also lived in a tent the previous summer and were featured in a homeless program on a Eugene TV station. They never saw the show when it aired.

Through the winter months they rented a small house. "It had no insulation and if the heat wasn't on, the temperature inside would drop in a short time." Marie's deep voice rushed through the words, leaving no distinction from one to another. Her long, thin fingers kept time with her voice by dancing along the table or fidgeting with a napkin left near her. Her fine, straight hair hung in a ponytail to her lower back. "They sold the house and gave us 15 days to move." Her large, brown eyes, sunken in her narrow, drawn face, looked quickly from the table to the ceiling or to others around the room, never focusing on any spot. "We went back to living in a tent near the river."

Mitch added, "It's not really like camping. I keep the campsite immaculate." He looked at Marie. "It is real important to her to have a house, somewhere to live." Between both their social security disability checks, affording a house would be difficult.

Marie had bi-polar and multi-personality disorders. Mitch worked to keep her away from situations that could trigger problems. She could change personalities instantly, a trait I soon witnessed.

"Genna has helped us a lot." Marie complimented the Soup Kitchen volunteer. "It was so good of her to open and run this Soup Kitchen."

"Genna is a wonderful person and works hard here, but the Soup Kitchen was running long before she came," I quietly corrected.

Marie's hands flew in front of her face, palms out and she shook her head. "I'm not going to get into this." She swiftly scooped up her things and marched out the door.

I looked at Mitch, who calmly remained in his chair. "I'm so sorry. I didn't mean to upset her," I apologized.

"That's just Marie." Mitch shrugged his shoulders. "Tell me about how the soup kitchen began."

Gladly, I told him how God worked through many people. "More people should know that," Mitch said as I finished the story. "You all deserve more recognition than you get."

"I wish there was more we could do," I said, thinking of the many needs of those around the room.

"This is a lot. Little things can mean so much." He smiled. "Like the shine in your eyes that shows to others." He stood and slid his chair up to the table. "Thanks."

I watched him walk away, telling others "good-bye" as he left. My attention shifted to the volunteers busy cleaning tables. None of them gave of their time for recognition. Knowing that someone appreciated their efforts was reward enough.

"Let us consider how we may spur one another on toward love and good deeds." Hebrews 10:24. The glow of one warm thought could do just that. I would pass the compliments on.

Mitch and Marie found a studio apartment to move into before the winter set in. I enjoyed visiting with Marie during meals, and even sat outside with her once after the Soup Kitchen was closed. She was upset and needed to talk. I didn't have any answers, just sat with her.

Marie's hair began to have a shine to it and she styled it different ways. Her rosy cheeks high-lighted her high cheekbones and her complexion tanned to accent her brown eyes. One evening she looked stunning as she arrived in an emerald green dress. I smiled, glad she was no longer hiding her natural beauty. That was another compliment I could pass on.

Sample Menu:
Meatloaf
Mashed Potatoes
Gravy
Green Beans
Green Salad
Apricots
Dessert

Frank Crowley, right, and Dan Wilkerson.

Merthal, Faye Hensley, manager, and Charlene

Photo by Nancey West
Norma on a Friday night.

Photo by Nancey West
Arnie with Roy Rogers t-shirt.

Courtesy of Soup Kitchen
Marge cutting hair.

Courtesy of Soup Kitchen
Melva and Joyce at a board meeting

Photo by Nancey West
Chuck serving coffee

Guests

Photos by Nancey West

Guests

Photos by Nancey West

Adding Compassion

Where there is great love there are always miracles.

Willa Cather

Bob and Zee are examples of how people created miracles by the love and compassion they gave. They attended the organizational meeting in the fireside room of the church and immediately became active in helping the Soup Kitchen take shape.

Bob was the church's property manager and was always busy with maintenance and repairs. Such work in the Soup Kitchen naturally fell to him. The electrical system needed upgrading before meals could be served. He took on the project of seeing it done properly. The job didn't stop at the electrical. There was always work for him to do with plumbing and handyman repairs.

Zee helped in the kitchen, learning from the cooks before cooking on her own. She teamed up with Joyce as coordinators to form a solid leadership for 13 years. Zee's job was to schedule the volunteers, write menus and cook, while Joyce kept inventory and ordered supplies.

"The volunteers are the community coming together." Zee's smile lit her face as she proudly talked of those offering their time and skills. "Cooks are all different. One cooked with a lot of rosemary. Another made spicy meals. Meals were always good. Even if they had to be dressed up, they always came out perfect."

One of the cooks asked Zee why she and Bob gave so many hours to the work of the Soup Kitchen. "Well, it is our mission," she explained in her soft, gentle voice.

One evening, as we drank tea in her kitchen, Zee reminisced of the experiences she and Bob had over their years of service.

They had a strong commitment in serving God by helping others. One of those they wanted to help was Mike. He was 15-years-old when his parents left him on the streets in Sweet Home and returned to California. He had several run-ins with the law and spent time in jail when he began eating at the Soup Kitchen. He arrived each night on his bike.

Mike's denim coat hung loose across his narrow shoulders. One evening, it opened in front enough to reveal a handgun tucked into his jeans. Zee called the police before she struck up a conversation with the dark-haired youth. Police arrived and took the high-powered BB gun from him without incident.

Another time, Mike managed to take keys out of the church office. Zee got word from other guests that Mike planned to return to the church that night to steal computers. Out of love, Bob and Zee wanted to prevent Mike from committing a crime. They waited outside of the church for Mike to arrive. "I was seeing if the Soup Kitchen was still open," Mike explained when he saw the couple waiting in the dark parking lot.

"You know it's not." Bob laughed. "We just want the keys returned." He held out his hand to Mike. Their own safety had not been considered until that moment as they waited for Mike's response. Zee remembered the handgun and wondered if Mike ever got it back.

While waiting for Mike's answer, a car quickly turned toward them, blinding them in the headlights. Two police officers stepped out of the car to question the trio and search Mike for weapons. They found a long pick concealed beneath his jacket.

One of the officers explained that a man who was to be Mike's accomplice had called the police to report a planned burglary. The officer also pointed out the danger that Bob and Zee had placed themselves in.

The police were not the only agency to be called for assistance. One summer a large fiftyish man in worn jeans and a dingy black coat came to eat his meal and always asked for two take-outs; one for his elderly mother and another for his disabled sister. He explained that both had difficulty getting in and out of the Volkswagen van, so they waited in the parking lot. The extra meals were always provided for the women. One evening, Zee offered to take food out to the women while the man ate. He insisted that she didn't need to.

This courtesy was not a problem for Zee and she happily carried the meals outside. Her cheerful smile quickly faded as she saw the filth in the interior of the van. The stench made her nearly drop the containers of food. The Health Department was called and the women taken to a cleaner environment.

Another meal occasionally served outside was for Big Bill. He was a middle aged likeable man who lived in his sister's garage. He was usually drunk, sometimes worse than others. If he was *too* drunk he would not go inside and Bob would serve him at the side of the church building. When he was sober enough, he stayed to mop the floors after his meal.

James was another regular guest who often had been drinking when he came to eat. One night, he came in drunk and crying that some kids threw all his possessions in the canal. He lost everything. Volunteers gave him clothes, toiletries and a sleeping bag. James was in need of a sleeping bag on several occasions and he was always supplied with one. Soon after that situation, he went to Serenity Lanes for alcohol treatment. After he became sober, he returned to the Soup Kitchen to share poetry he wrote. People were drawn to him because they could relate to the personal struggles he talked about.

Clothes were kept for such emergencies as James's or Denny's. Denny was an American Indian who came in lugging a large, black tote bag over his stooped shoulders. With his head down, he carried his load to the back of the dining hall and sat it on the floor near the wall. His long, black hair was threaded with silver, matching the speckles in his beard and mustache. His rich complexion could not hide the years of weathering the outdoor elements. He was a regular during the summer months but went to California for the winter. In nearly every type of weather he could be found in his long, black trench coat, dirty jeans and an Army shirt. He could often be found sleeping on the steps at the Catholic Church. The story was told that at one time he was a barber but didn't like the work and adopted a lifestyle on the streets.

One evening Denny came in drenched from the heavy rains during the day and was in need of dry clothes and a new bag. The clothes were always available but rarely was there a bag or backpack. Miracles do occur though. Earlier that day someone brought in a large duffel bag that was just the size Denny needed. He appreciated the unexpected gift and tried to say so. His thick, heavy voice was hard to understand but his grin told it all.

Pete was a similar story. He lived at Waterloo and regularly walked or hitched a ride the seven miles to the Soup Kitchen. One night he arrived cold and wet, looking for only a warm meal and a dry place to sit. When he was given all new clothes, he bounced with excitement. "Thank you, thank you," he repeated, nearly laughing.

Not everyone who came in laughed. Charlotte, a thin, weathered lady, came in one evening crying. Between heaving sobs, she explained that her 12-year-old son just died of a brain tumor. Sympathy flowed from the compassionate volunteers for her devastating loss. Several tried to comfort her with hugs and gentle words of sorrow. She lingered after her meal as Zee and others visited with her.

She did not return to the Soup Kitchen for several nights and Zee became concerned for her well-being. Zee asked other guests if they knew her until she found some of Charlotte's friends. She told them of her concern for Charlotte after her heart-breaking loss. Zee was shocked to learn that Charlotte never had a son.

It was common not to know about a guest's life outside the dining hall. A man in his twenties with a broken arm came in several times. One evening he arrived early and Zee greeted him with a smile and a hug. She didn't know anything about him or how he had been injured. Three months later he returned to the Soup Kitchen. He found Zee to tell her, "You saved my life because you cared. I was going to end it. Then you gave me that hug." That simple sign of compassion gave him the strength to find a job and begin improving his life.

It was not always possible to know how caring acts at the Soup Kitchen affected someone. A young woman with tear-stained cheeks arrived one night with a baby on her hip and two small girls following closely. Her voice cracked with desperation as she explained that her husband had just kicked her out. While they ate, volunteers found shoes and clothes for the kids in the storage room. They fixed lunches for the discarded family and took them to a local motel for the night. We never saw them again.

Other agencies were often contacted to provide more help and, like the above rejected young mother, Soup Kitchen volunteers never learned what happened to them.

Bob and Zee's mission could be found described in I Thessalonians 2:11-12, "For you know that we dealt with each of you as a father deals with his own children, encouraging, comforting and urging you to live lives worthy of God."

Compassion was a driving force in giving so much of one's life to charity. Zee and Bob's mission was who they were. They couldn't live without giving. Miracles happened because of the love they gave.

Sample Menu:
Pizza
Pasta Salad
Green Salad
Chocolate-Banana Pudding
Dessert

Courtesy of Zee Hauck
Bob and Zee

Adjusting the Heat

Since we cannot change reality, let us change the eyes which see reality.

Nikos Kazantzakis

Buckets of donated ripe, red cherries were scattered around the kitchen. "I can think of a lot of things to make with them," one of the cooks said as she began frying hamburger for the evening meal. "But I don't have time to pit them."

"Neither do I," another, cutting lettuce, agreed.

Marcy, the coordinator of the Soup Kitchen, read down the list of volunteers, "We need someone who isn't already helping." She sat the list down and paused before calling Joyce Dart. Joyce attended the First Christian Church and had not opposed establishing the Soup Kitchen, but made it known she didn't want anything to do with it.

After a long silence, Joyce firmly answered Marcy's plea for help, "I'll do it if I'm not around those people who come."

"You won't be," Marcy assured her. "Come in when you can."

Joyce entered the kitchen early the next day, when the cooks weren't there, and began the process of cleaning and pitting the succulent fruit. Hours later, with crimson hands and red-stained clothes, she finished her job and cleaned the juicy mess from the counter.

The next time she was asked to help, Joyce still felt reluctance. "I guess I can wash pots, as long as…."

"You'll be working in the kitchen. You won't need to go into the dining area," Marcy interrupted to reassure her, again.

"I'll be there," the third grade teacher confirmed.

89

Joyce arrived the next evening while the cooks were finishing preparations to serve the meal. "I'm glad you came," Marcy whispered as she led Joyce to the dining area. "We always pray before we open the doors," she quickly responded to Joyce's look of concern at being escorted out of the kitchen.

As soon as "Amen" was said, Joyce retreated to the stack of pots on the counter just inside the kitchen door. The sink was only a few feet away from the serving counter, leaving Joyce uneasily close to the people as they received their food. The sanitizer, similar to a dishwasher, was next to the sink, allowing her to fill it with her back toward the door. Not facing the guests offered a small amount of comfort.

Washing pots became a routine for Joyce. "How are you tonight?" She'd greet others as she arrived from her day filled with children.

"Something smells good," she sucked in the steaming aroma from a kettle on the stove deep in her nostrils.

"It's always good," the cook verified with a chuckle.

"I'm sure it is," Joyce smiled and began filling the sink with hot, soapy water. Used pots and mixing bowls crowded the counter. Joyce began washing as others arraigned food in the serving line.

While setting the bread in the warmer one cook asked, "Joyce, can you help serve tonight? We are short-handed."

The light slipped from her brown eyes and the corners of her smiling mouth fell. The serving counter was only a few steps from her comfortable station at the sink, where she faced only her task. Serving would mean facing the guests as they came through the line. The other volunteers needed help and she was standing right there. How could she refuse?

"As long as I'm not out there," she said, pointing toward the empty tables in the dining hall.

"Good. You can serve the vegetable and bread and hand the plate to Debbie." The cook explained the simple process as they washed their hands.

Joyce slipped rubber gloves on and began filling plates in the assembly line. "Would you like bread?" She softly asked each recipient, while intently keeping her eyes on her work. When she glanced up, the faces looking back startled her. She saw smiles and heard an occasional "How ya doin'?" They were not all the sad, down-trodden expressions she expected. Curiously, she studied the line of patiently waiting guests, many who were visiting with each other. The edges of her rigid lips softened. The people she referred to as "those people out there" looked like ordinary people. Some looked happy and friendly. Some looked worn and tired. Some were neatly dressed. Others wore tattered clothes. They all held their own story.

Her voice became warmer. "Would you like bread?" A smile slowly crept across her hardened face, softening the wrinkles around her squinted eyes.

Handing out food gave her a new way to serve God. With encouraging words she greeted guests. "God gave you such beautiful eyes," she complimented a heavyset young woman. "That blue sure looks good on you," she told another.

Joyce began helping with inventory and learning to order needed items and continued to serve meals. "Why don't you come to the board meeting tonight?" Marcy asked one day while they were stacking items in the small storage room. Seeing the familiar reluctance in Joyce's face, Marcy continued, "The meeting is right after we clean up. You might as well stay."

She stayed and was voted as a new board member. Her dedication and love for the Soup Kitchen grew as she spent more time volunteering. She and Zee, another volunteer from the First Christian Church, were soon working together in managing the Soup Kitchen. Zee was a cook and oversaw the work in the kitchen, scheduled cooks and wrote menus. Joyce placed the orders, took inventory and recorded donations.

Joyce later commented, "We worked together so long, we knew what each other were thinking."

Four months after pitting cherries, Joyce took the position of chair of the board when I resigned in November 1989.

After retiring from teaching, Joyce volunteered more time at the Soup Kitchen. Serving desserts was her favorite because she stood next to the door to the dining room; the door she used to keep her back towards. Occasionally, she would step into the dining room to give someone a hug.

Joyce watched as a slender lady with deep lines around her reddened eyes pointed to a donut. "You look like you could use a hug," Joyce said, handing her the pastry.

Moisture ran down the lady's dark face as Joyce put her arms around her. "God hates me," she said, trembling with tears.

"God doesn't hate you," Joyce softly assured her.

"Then why did He take my children?" Anger flowed in her deep, raspy voice.

"Child Services did not take your children because God hates you. He loves you," Joyce tried comforting the woman as she left with her tray.

Another evening, a rugged, middle-aged man slid his tray along the counter. He took his plate and moved to the dessert window. Suddenly, he shouted, "Joyce!"

Joyce's face lit with excitement when she recognized the gentlemen. "Roy, you haven't been around in a long time." She stepped through the door to give him a hug.

"Did you notice I lost 100 pounds?" he turned around to show off his thin body.

"Yes, I did. I've lost weight too, but only 70 pounds."

"You look great and it's good to see you still working here." He said as he left with his tray.

Joyce remained a constant part of the Soup Kitchen life through the years. In 2002, a manager was hired to do many of the things that Joyce and Zee had been doing. That did not diminish her presence. She continued to help with ordering food, receiving donations and serving meals. Years in front of a classroom left her at ease when talking with organizations and groups concerning the needs and services of the Soup Kitchen. She worked hard on getting grants, supplies and services for the addition that was so great a need. The place she wanted to avoid became her passion.

Travel was another passion. After retiring from the Lebanon School District, she and her husband, Ed, joined Friendship Force. They traveled to many countries and hosted people from foreign countries in their home. Some of their guests helped in the Soup Kitchen during their stay.

They also joined an RV group for camping and traveling. Some trips took months to complete. Every year they took their RV to Arizona to stay for the winter, officially becoming "snow-birds."

Each adventure took Joyce away from the daily activity of the Soup Kitchen. She left the work in good hands and remained easily accessible by phone or email. She did not see God's vision in the beginning but her eyes were opened to a new reality. She heard God calling her to years of dedicated service. She was surely blessed as Matthew 12:16 said, "blessed are your eyes because they see, and your ears because they hear."

Sample Menu:
Hot Dogs
Chips
Pork-n-beans
Cabbage Slaw
Peaches

Courtesy of Zee Hauck
Joyce

Kneads a Promise

God hears the faintest cry of the sick, the lonely,
the despised of the world.
And He cares—deeply—about each one.

Dr. James Dobson

Many people make a pact with God when they are in a seemingly hopeless situation. "I will dedicate my life to you, God, if You help me now," they cry. When the crisis is over, they forget the deal.

Genna Foster was not one of those people. When she was diagnosed with cancer she told God, "If I can get through this, I will work for you." He heard her cry, and she kept her promise.

After she completed treatment and the cancer was in remission, she asked God to show her where He wanted her to serve. She thought of volunteering at a school but after 22 years as a secretary at Linn Benton Community College, she wanted something different.

One afternoon she saw Grace Johnson, a Soup Kitchen board member, loading donated bread into the back of her van outside one of the local grocery stores. Genna was curious and struck up a conversation. Volunteering at the Soup Kitchen sparked an interest and she asked how to help. It was a way for her to fulfill James 1:27, "Religion that God our Father accepts as pure and faultless is this: to look after orphans and widows in their distress and to keep oneself from being polluted by the world."

Genna began washing dishes, pots and pans every Monday, Wednesday and Friday night at the Soup Kitchen. Sweat formed on her brow as steam filled the cramped kitchen each time she opened the sanitizer's door but she was satisfied with the work God gave her. She was comfortable being unnoticed in the kitchen and away from the activities in the dining hall.

Genna quickly became friends with the manager, Faye, and was at ease with the other volunteers. "Do you have any secretarial skills?" Faye asked her one day, not aware of her long history in the field. "The Soup Kitchen board needs a secretary."

Reluctant to return to clerical work, Genna declined the offer. Later, she reconsidered the opportunity to help and accepted the position.

During meals, she spent an increasing amount of time visiting with the guests and helping clear tables, until she gave up washing dishes. She dedicated a lot of energy to the Soup Kitchen and its guests. "Because I have the time, I give 110%," Genna explained her dedication.

While gathering plates in the dining room, she monitored the activity for inappropriate language or actions. Such as when a shapely blond wearing a canary yellow halter top and tight-fitting shorts, joined her friends at a table. The young woman sat down and her scantily fitting clothes left her lower back exposed. Genna handed her a button-up shirt, kept in the closet for such occasions. "No one wants to see your crack while eating," her deep voice was firm. Hesitantly, the young lady slipped the shirt on.

Genna's help often went beyond serving meals. She also looked for ways to help individual needs, like the grey-haired man in dingy denim jeans, cut off at the tops of his heavy work boots, who introduced himself as Kelly. He extended a tanned and weathered hand as he rolled up the sleeves of his black and grey hickory shirt. He explained he was looking for work in the woods. Genna smiled, "There is someone here you should talk to." Soon I returned to the table with her. Because of my forestry background, she hoped I would be able to steer him toward contacts for work.

Genna did what she could and sometimes more than she planned. For example, Lens Crafters in Salem offered free glasses to anyone with a prescription and a letter from a non-profit organization stating their need for financial help. Genna passed the information around during soup kitchen meals. Four men asked to participate. One did not have a prescription. Genna called a local optometrist and the man received a free exam and his needed prescription.

On the day the free glasses were offered, the men arranged to meet and ride with the only one of them who had a vehicle. Genna wrote the reference letters and drove to the Soup Kitchen to give them to the men. When she arrived at the Soup Kitchen parking lot, there sat four middle-aged, homeless men and no vehicle. Their only mode of transportation would not start that morning.

Genna knew the opportunity for the needed eyewear would not wait. "Pile in," she motioned toward her own car. The half-hour drive to Salem was filled with stories, laughter and song.

The men were fitted for glasses and told it would be five hours before they would be ready. Five hours! By this time, Genna's quick-trip-to-the-soup-kitchen-parking-lot had become an all-day adventure.

The group continued their stories at a nearby buffet, over a two-hour lunch provided by Genna. By the end of the long day of waiting, each had his pair of free glasses.

Another time, Genna received a phone call from a man in Corvallis who was tearing down an old motel. He offered her first choice of anything she wanted, if she could pick it up within two days. The items offered were just what she needed for her dream of opening a homeless shelter in Lebanon. Genna needed help to pick them up.

During the Wednesday evening meal, Genna asked if any of the guests at the Soup Kitchen could help move the items to a storage unit she had reserved. She rented a U-Haul truck for the next morning, without knowing if anyone would actually show up to help. When she arrived at the Soup Kitchen, 15 men with five pickups were waiting in the parking lot. The small caravan drove to the motel in Corvallis. The men loaded the truck in 45 minutes with twin beds, roll-away beds, TVs, dressers, lamps, tables, linens, pillows and blankets.

The owner of the motel was so impressed with the men's effort that he let them load their pickups with anything they could personally use. When the group finished, they had removed items from a section of one wing in the motel, leaving much more for other non-profit organizations to use.

Genna was serious about helping people who came to the Soup Kitchen, but she often joked with many of them during meals. Stan was one of them. He always sat at the end of the third table next to Bob. Stan wore an old army hat that he took off inside the building and carefully sat it on the table near him. Genna playfully grabbed it and hurried away. Stan would usually hop to his feet to chase her. On other nights he just yelled for her to bring it back. Genna returned the hat and they laughed.

When Stan died unexpectedly at home, Genna attended his funeral and told the hat story. She explained he was a regular visitor to the Soup Kitchen, where his company was enjoyed by many. The hat was in Stan's hands as he lay in the casket. Genna thought how fitting that was. Following the service, Stan's son found Genna. "I think it would be fitting for you to have this," he gently placed the hat in Genna's hand.

After Stan had missed several meals, Bob questioned Genna on where his friend was. "Who's your friend?" Genna asked. "I don't know his name," Bob snapped. "He sat here." Bob pointed to the vacant seat next to him. Genna told Bob the sad news of his nameless friend.

Genna sometimes made handing out food to take home entertaining. Leftover food from one night was divided into small containers and given out during the next meal. The same was done with sandwiches and pizza donated by businesses. While guests were eating, Genna pushed a cart filled with the to-go packages down the wide isle between tables. "Get your hotdogs here," she called out, imitating a vendor at a ball game. "Hotdogs. Get your hotdogs." People joined in the fun, calling back, "over here," or "I'll take one." One raised his arm and yelled above the others, "A dog and a beer!" Everyone laughed at the suggestion of serving a beer at the Soup Kitchen.

Genna gave of herself and her resources to other guests. Arlene lived down the road from her and never drove, so Genna gave Arlene a ride to the Soup Kitchen and to many of her doctor appointments. She even sat in the waiting room through Arlene's surgery and visited her often at Lebanon Rehab.

Not all her compassionate stories had happy endings. Sometimes they were painful, such as Vicky, a regular visitor who lived nearby. She was repeatedly hospitalized for alcoholism. Genna went to see her at the Lebanon Hospital each time she was admitted. Along with others, Genna would encourage Vicky to go to a recovery clinic, but she would become angry and often leave the hospital without checking out. Vicky would return to her small apartment and her drinking. Eventually, she could no longer take care of herself and was moved to a care facility in Corvallis.

Another sad case was Fred's. Fred began as a success story. He was a quiet man. His fair skin and rosy cheeks peeked out above his bushy red beard, while his long, red hair was pulled into a tight ponytail. He was homeless but unlike many in his situation, he was not haunted with an addiction. He eagerly agreed to the rules of the newly formed Lebanon Shelter and was one of its first residents.

One evening, he was not feeling well so the manager of the shelter took him to the hospital. He was treated for double pneumonia but succumbed to complications. Notifying Fred's family proved to be a task. He had two sisters but only their names were known, not a city or state in which to locate them. Friends he hung out with at the park said he had an ex-wife and three children, but no one knew names. Some thought they lived locally. Notices were placed in most of the convenient stores in the area, in hopes that some relative would come forward. A son saw the notice at the Waterloo Store and called the number. Fred's family, including his sisters, was located.

Genna also dedicated time in raising funds and awareness for the Soup Kitchen. She taped information about the Soup Kitchen on cans with a slot in the lid and asked for change. For two years she placed the cans in many stores around town and collected several thousand dollars in change. One can was stolen from Bing's Restaurant and the owner replaced the stolen money with much more than what would have been collected in the can. Genna wrote a letter to the editor of the local paper and scolded whoever had stolen the can and how sad it was to steal from those who feed the poor. Soon after the letter appeared, an anonymous donor sent $300 to the Soup Kitchen.

Besides opening her heart, Genna and her husband, Will, open their home for foreign exchange students. Some have lived with them for a school year while others stayed only for a weekend. Genna enjoys entertaining people and showing them the beauty of our area. Many of them have experienced the work of the Soup Kitchen while they lived with her.

Genna joyfully kept her promise to God to serve Him. She sees the needs of others and deeply cares about helping them.

Sample Menu:
Taco Salad
Chips
Cheese/sour cream/jalapenos
Jell-O Salad
Dessert

Photo by Jon West
Genna and Nancey greeting
guests at Christmas

Sifting Differences

It is not the level of prosperity that makes for happiness but the kinship of heart to heart and the way we look at the world that knits us together.

Russian writer, Aleksandr Solzhenitsyn

Merthal never knew what it was like to be homeless. She never experienced the uncertainty of where her next meal would come from. She never slept in the cold and rain with only cardboard and brush for protection.

Merthal wore designer clothes accented with beautiful jewelry, lived in a lovely home and drove a Mercedes. That was Merthal and that's the way she came to the Soup Kitchen.

In earlier years, she and her husband, Carroll, enjoyed square dancing and motorcycle riding, when they weren't working in their plant nursery. Merthal enjoyed sewing and made many of the family's clothes. She was active in several organizations, such as the Rebecca's. After selling the nursery, the couple moved into Lebanon.

When Carroll died, Merthal stopped eating. She asked to be called Carroll, instead of her own name. Grief and loneliness filled her time.

Friends became worried. Karen, a friend from one of the many organizations she was a member of, insisted she go to the Soup Kitchen. Merthal resisted the idea.

"Either you go or I will take you," Karen threatened.

"All right," her dark eyes narrowed as she reluctantly agreed.

The two women came to the Soup Kitchen together. They ate quickly and left. They came again, sat alone and hurried away.

"Good evening," smiling faces greeted them each night. "How are you doing tonight?" a lady asked as she sat beside the two women. The friendly exchanges encouraged the two to linger after their meal. When Karen stopped coming, Merthal continued, finding more people to visit. The "welcome" she received wasn't just in the words, but in the uplifting voices and tender gestures. She felt a sense of belonging and often stayed until all the work was done.

A lady with short, grey hair cleared and wiped tables as they talked. "You are welcome to help anytime," she suggested during one conversation.

Merthal's long, thin fingers, wrinkled with age, gripped a spatula to wipe plates as she joined the volunteers. The edges of her pink lips lifted her rosy checks and a sparkle glistened in her dark eyes nestled behind wire-rimmed glasses. Visitors returned her smile.

Prayer was important to her and she started arriving early to join the volunteers. Warm words of encouragement drew her close with many of the volunteers, especially Faye, the manager.

"I want to be on the board," she announced one evening. The next meeting, she was voted to the board where her contributions were welcome.

"You should leave your expensive jewelry at home," a volunteer suggested one night while admiring a shiny broach.

She ignored the advice with the explanation, "They all know me here." She felt comfortable among the poor. She treated them with friendliness and compassion and trusted them to return her respect. Barely seeing over the steering wheel, she was always ready to give someone a ride home.

Over the years, her tall, thin frame would no longer stand straight and she needed the help of a cane to walk. Her years of volunteering came to an end, but not her participation in each meal.

Quietly, she told Helen, a cook, "If you ever need anything, let me know." Merthal was always ready to give back to the place that she had become a part of. Her generous gifts were to remain anonymous. She gave from her heart for the interest of others, as found in Philippians 2:3-5, "Do nothing out of selfish ambition or vain conceit, but in humility consider others better than yourselves. Each of you should look not only to your own interest, but also to the interests of others."

A friend was looking out for her interest, when he offered to give her a ride on his new Vespa. The large scooter wasn't like the motorcycles from her younger years, but remembering the thrill of the wind blowing in her face sparked a light in her eyes.

"Where would you like to go?" He asked.

"Go wherever someone can see me," she said, settling the large helmet over her head.

The ride around town and country roads did not take her past many onlookers who recognized her behind the husky man. She made up for the lack of attention at the next Soup Kitchen meal by recounting her evening adventure to all her friends. Excitement bubbled in her voice each time she told the story.

Over the years, the cooks learned which foods Merthal couldn't eat or didn't like. When those dishes were served they made something special to slip to her as she came through the line.

"Getting to know Merthal was one of the highlights of my life," beamed a volunteer.

She could afford her own food. What she couldn't afford was the solitude and loneliness of her empty home. The work and people of the Soup Kitchen filled her aching heart.

"If it wasn't for the Soup Kitchen, I'd stepped out in front of a truck a long time ago," she told Joyce, a volunteer, one evening. "I have felt love here that I never felt before."

The appreciation was mutual. The kinship of their hearts had knit them together. The day of the dedication for the new addition to the Soup Kitchen happened to be her 88th birthday. She was presented with a plaque:

Certificate of Appreciation
Merthal Settlemier
In appreciation of her Christian love and dedication, and for her
generous and faithful contributions
The Lebanon Soup Kitchen
recognizes our most cherished quest.
Given on this 11th day of June in the year 2005

Sample Menu:
Fried Chicken
Green Beans
Buttered Bread
Potato Salad
Cantaloupe
Dessert

Cuts Habits

To many, total abstinence is easier than perfect moderation.

St. Augustine

Sherrill parked her bicycle next to the flowering tree in the Soup Kitchen parking lot and snapped the lock in place. She ambled through the kitchen, greeting others along the way. There was nearly half an hour until serving started which gave her time to hang up her coat, visit with friends and wash her hands before beginning her nightly routine of filling the juice glasses. A few minutes before prayer time, she poured the milk. The glasses lined the top of a tall table that was rimmed with sides the same height as the glasses to prevent the beverages from spilling to the floor. The drinks could easily be handed to guests as they left the serving line to enjoy their meal.

Sherrill first came to the Soup Kitchen with the encouragement of her friend, Cindy. "She brought people to the Soup Kitchen when they lost someone or were down. She was a pick-me-up for many people." She bragged of her friend's compassion. "I had hit bottom in life and was depressed. I was satisfied to just live on baloney. But Cindy, Doris and others encouraged me to come to the Soup Kitchen." She pointed to some women visiting at a nearby table in the dining hall. "Coming here gave me three meals a week, and when I was feeling down, I came in just to be in the company of people. I became a regular. I was glad to help anywhere I could. The Soup Kitchen allowed me to feel a part of community, my extended family."

One day while peeling potatoes, Sherrill was listening to a lady sent for Community Service work complain about a class she was required to take for her drinking problem. "She didn't like the questions they asked, like, 'How

103

important is drinking to you?' Without remembering where I was, I said "It was everything and cost me everything." I was picturing my own battle with alcohol but suddenly realized I had spoken out loud and the people around me heard." Her blue eyes widened. "My past was no longer a secret."

Her positive attitude brought a smile. "Things work out though. I visited with the lady who was complaining and she went to a 12-step recovery program with me. She later brought her family to the meetings. During one visit, she told me of an adult foster home that was looking for help. I inquired and got the job. The lady I went to work for talked her sister-in-law into joining Alcoholics Anonymous. That "everything" statement that I blurted out opened the door for all of us to get help."

Sherrill became an alcoholic years ago. "Reality had caused me to stub my toe. I couldn't meet life on life's terms. Life seemed overwhelming, something that I didn't get. It overwhelmed me like an ocean wave. I was always suicidal."

Her second marriage was dissolving, when Sherrill, at age 33, began drinking. But she started attending Ala-non for the benefit of her then-husband. He had grown up in an apartment above a grocery store and worked in the store when young. His efforts were rewarded with beer, so he began drinking at age six. Since he had been drinking for so long, Sherrill was convinced that he was the one with the problem. She did not see she had a problem until after she participated in Ala-non for two years.

A bartender and several friends at the Eagles suggested that Sherrill join AA. She denied she was the one with the problem. "Then I met with people in AA and decided I wanted what they had, but in order to get it I had to stop drinking."

Then her first granddaughter was born weighing only three and a half pounds. Sherrill bargained with God that if He let the little girl live, she would improve her life. "My granddaughter gave me something to love enough to face my own alcohol problem. I joined AA and never returned to the Eagles. The 12-step program was my lifeline. Going there I began to see God has a big family. It opened my heart and mind to something bigger than this world. It gave me spiritual opening." Twenty-seven years later she was still in the program. "When on the 12-step program you are never on safe turf. You can't look past today. You have to look to do God's glory daily. It is a life or death deal."

A local man, who volunteered in the serving line, developed a rapport with many guests in the 12-step program. He often came in when not serving to encourage them to remain sober. "He helped me when I was down," Sherrill said.

Feeling a part of the community helped Sherrill build the courage to daily commit to remaining sober.

Not all alcoholics have a successful ending. Valerie lived in the apartment across the hall from Sherrill. Her dark hair hung tangled over her wide shoulders. She supported her tall frame with a cane that made a hollow-sounding "thump" each time it connected with the wooden floor of the dining hall. A sword hidden inside the cane gave it the unusual sound.

"They have good food here," she told me one day when I visited with her during a meal. "The Soup Kitchen has helped me out. I live on food stamps and when they get low, I come here. I live upstairs and in the summer it gets too hot to cook."

Quietly she told me her rocky path to Lebanon. "I am from Texas. My ex-husband was driving a cross-country truck. He asked me to go with him." She shifted in the hard metal chair. "That was fine until he beat me up and left me for dead along the road." She silently stared at the food remaining on her plate. Moisture filled her brown eyes as she continued. "When I recovered, I was stuck in Michigan with no family or friends. My ex-husband's brother paid for a train ticket for me to come to Oregon. He said he would help me but he ended up being just like his brother."

She looked around the busy dining hall. "I have no family and nowhere to go. These people are my family now, especially Bulldog. He keeps an eye on me." Later I discovered she had a son in the Marines. He had invited her to live with him but she did not go.

Valerie's long arms looked like matchsticks and her narrow face became sunken. When she was not strong enough to walk the two blocks to the Soup Kitchen, Sherrill took boxed meals to her.

"I wanted to help her because she was my daughter's age." Frustration rang in Sherrill's voice. Sherrill became uncomfortable with the deliveries when Valerie began carrying a pistol. "Valerie easily became irrational, yelling and making false accusations towards neighbors. She would go outside naked and walk around or relax in one of the chairs on the sidewalk. Neighbors called the police but Valerie dressed by the time they arrived."

Because of her drinking, several times Valerie was admitted to the hospital. Each time, the hospital staff suggested that she go to a treatment center. She routinely refused and called someone to take her home.

One evening Valerie called the Soup Kitchen to ask if Sherrill would bring her some food. The volunteer taking the call knew Sherrill had done so on several occasions and said okay to the request. This time Sherrill explained her concerns in Valerie's changing personality. Two volunteers, Joe and Pete, reluctantly agreed to deliver the meal. They hesitated in the hallway outside Valerie's apartment for a short prayer before knocking on the door. A raspy voice snapped, "Come in." Slowly Joe eased the door open and stepped in to the dark room. Valerie was sitting in a recliner with two revolvers on her lap. Joe set the meal on a table beside her and asked if he could pray with her. Gently he placed his hand on her shoulder and offered a prayer. Valerie thanked him, her eyes reddened with emotion.

"There are three things that can happen when you are an alcoholic." Sherrill explained. "1. You can get sober. 2. You can die. Or 3. You can be admitted to a mental institute for insanity. That's what we call wetbrain." The Bible confirms number three in Hosea 4:11, "Alcohol has robbed people of their brains." (New Living Translation)

Valerie's condition continued to decline. She stayed alone in her apartment and stopped smoking and drinking alcohol. Not long afterwards, she stopped eating and drinking water. Again, she was taken to a local hospital with complications of alcoholism. Several people from the Soup Kitchen visited her before she was transferred to a care facility in Corvallis. Sherrill sent her a card signed "all your friends from the Soup Kitchen." Valerie never returned.

Sample Menu:
Chicken Nuggets
Potato Wedges
Carrots
Garlic Bread
Green Salad
Jell-O Salad
Dessert

Bubbles Over

In this life we cannot do great things.
We can only do small things with great love.

Mother Teresa

A new pink sweater, the collar and cuffs rimmed in fluffy, pink fur, sat on the bench in the foyer of the church. It looked as if it were waiting for a tiny ice skater to wrap it around her shoulders and sail through twirls and pirouettes in a dazzling display of fancy footwork. The soft garment looked out of place among the worn and wrinkled clothing displayed for the guests to choose.

Thanksgiving neared and the temperatures outside decreased. Patty and her daughter, Cindy, sat out stacks of warm clothes when the sweater caught Cindy's attention. The special sweater needed to go to someone who would appreciate its unique beauty. Cindy carefully tucked the sweater away as she planned her search for the perfect recipient.

Guests arrived and rummaged through the offering of clothes. Some eagerly examined the items before they got their food. Others casually waited until they had finished eating. The evening wore on and Cindy had not found that special person.

Towards the end of the evening, when most guests had come and gone, Cindy saw her. A little girl about seven years old fidgeted in her chair next to her mom and her two brothers. Cindy retrieved the sweater and waited in the foyer.

Oh! Here they come! In her excitement, Cindy's heart tingled like a million butterflies dancing around it. She eagerly called the little girl over and asked her to turn around. "Let's see if this will fit you," Cindy said as she held the sweater against the girl's back.

"What is it?" The girl wiggled with curiosity.

"Oh, yes, it will fit perfectly," Cindy said as she slowly revealed the sweater.

"Oh!" The astonished child gasped as she studied the beautiful sweater. Ever so gently she touched the soft fur floating around the collar and sleeves like little pink clouds. "For me?" she softly questioned.

"Yes, for you." Cindy handed her the new sweater. "And it will look so beautiful on you."

"Thank you," she sighed, reaching for the hanger with such delicacy and grace. Her small arm held the sweater away from her body as if she might somehow damage it. She turned toward the dining area like a great artist to her audience and began her song of joy.

"Look at my gift. Isn't it beautiful? It's mine! It's my present! It fits me! See how pretty it is?" Over and over she sang her song with pride, making sure no one missed her serenade.

Stars sparkled in her glowing eyes, melting the hearts of those who watched her with awe. Her radiant face of thanksgiving and joy seemed to explode and fill the eyes of all those watching her. People who had come wrapped in hopelessness, anger or despair, now stood smiling. *Surely children are a gift from the Lord.* Psalms 127:3 tells us, "Sons are a heritage from the Lord, children a reward from him.

Tears filled Patty's eyes as she watched and thought of her grandchildren. "I thanked God for all their blessings for I knew each one had everything they needed. They had clothes in excess, shoes for every season, a roof over their heads and no worries about when their next meal may be." As the little girl wrapped in pink twirled around and around through the room, Patty made a commitment. She would use part of the money meant for her family's Christmas gifts and make a donation in their names to a charity that feeds, clothes and provides help and shelter to those in need in their area, the Phoenix Rescue Mission.

Patty wanted to remember the feelings the night she watched a little blonde enjoy a moment of happiness in receiving something special. "I made each of my family a Christmas decoration to keep the *Pink Sweater* story in mind and remember the needs of little girls and boys who are less fortunate."

Part of the note she wrote her family said, "I love you all very much, and pray that this year, you will each be filled with spiritual blessings above all other gifts and that not a day goes by that you don't make time to give thanks to God who, through your parents, has so blessed you with providing for all your needs."

Sample Menu:
Macaroni and Cheese
Green Salad
Buttered Bread
Peaches
Dessert

Secret Ingredient

One of the most valuable lessons (writing) has taught me is that it is in the smallest details that the flavor of life is savored.

Sarah Ban Breathnach,

By the time Claudette was seven months old she had been removed from her parents' home three times for dehydration and malnutrition. The tiny girl developed rickets and was left mentally handicapped. She was eventually placed in foster care and spent her early life moving from one foster home to another. Because of her disabilities, in many homes her physical and emotional care were neglected and in others she was abused.

One family, Stevens, left her with fond memories. They died when Claudette was young. She referred to anyone with the last name of Stevens as her family, though her birth name was Weeks.

At age 13, Claudette was sent to live in Fairview Home. The only information concerning her biological family to follow her through many moves was that she was of Klamath Indian heritage, had an older brother and that her father had been hit by a train when she was 2 years old.

Claudette never attended school but when she was older held menial jobs such as cleaning hotel rooms and sorting items at a local thrift store. Her limited vocabulary and many health issues, including diabetes and hypertension, restricted her ability to earn regular wages. However, for a short time she was able to support herself while living in a group home.

In 1992, she moved to a group home in Lebanon and then to Cambridge House in Albany in 1996.

Melinda, one of the support staff at Cambridge House, was an energetic woman with a compassionate heart who took a special interest in Claudette. Melinda found headstones in a nearby cemetery with the name Stevens engraved on them. Claudette visited the graves as if they were family and found comfort in regularly decorating them with flowers purchased from her meager budget.

Claudette cheerfully talked with other residents, staff and visitors. Her wide smile accented her high cheekbones and deep, rich eyes. Her long, grey hair enriched her bronze skin as she entertained the staff with one of her games. She dropped a dust cloth she was using and picked it up only to drop it again. "Butterfingers," she laughed, continuing the game as long as someone would watch.

The unknown years of Claudette's youth were filled in with her own imagination. She eagerly told stories of her family's activities and the fun they had together. If anyone questioned her, she admitted the truth of her past; but most of those who knew her allowed her to enjoy a moment of pleasure with the illusion.

Melinda, with the help of her manager, began searching for a connection to Claudette's past. Any Indian Melinda encountered would be quizzed on their heritage. The few Klamath Indians she met were not familiar with the Weeks family name.

Three nights a week, Melinda left her staff job at Cambridge House to serve at the Lebanon Soup Kitchen. Early in 2007, an Indian with peppered, shoulder-length hair began coming to the Soup Kitchen. Melinda's husband, Bruce, befriended many of the homeless men, and the quiet Indian, Darren, was no exception. At Melinda's constant urging, Bruce asked Darren if he was Klamath Indian. He was. Did he know anyone named Weeks? He did. After hearing the reason for the search, Darren offered to bring phone numbers of the family he knew in Klamath Falls.

Each night Darren arrived at the Soup Kitchen, Melinda would bubble with excitement in anticipation of receiving the magical numbers that would connect Claudette to her past. Her optimism never diminished each time Darren forgot the phone numbers. She reminded him again and waited until the next night. Finally, Darren brought the sought-after numbers.

The next day, Melinda anxiously called the number. A polite woman, Bonnie, answered the phone and listened to Melinda's story. She gave Melinda another number. The next call was to Irene in Chiloquin. The 57-year old said she had heard she had an older sister. The conversation confirmed Claudette was that sister. "Seek and you will find," (Matthew 7:7) Melinda laughed about her answered prayer.

Melinda's seven-year search finally ended. Claudette giggled with delight when she learned of her biological family. At age 62, she talked to the sister she never knew existed. She learned that their father had been killed by a train when Claudette was six years old, not two years old as she had always thought. Irene did not know the where-about of their 64-year-old brother, Larry.

Claudette waited for arrangements to be made for the two half-sisters to meet. She was eager to buy a doll for her "little" sister. Melinda sat her in front of a mirror to look at herself. Her little sister, Melinda explained, may look similar and probably didn't need a doll.

In late spring, Melinda and Bruce, and Melinda's boss, took Claudette, along with another resident, Robert, to Chiloquin. Their car pulled in front of a run-down house and Ilene could be seen watching out the window. She waved to Claudette before going to the door.

"Hi, little sister," Claudette called, her face beaming with delight. The two embraced as they met.

"It was obvious they were related," Melinda reflected of the similar appearance.

Bruce and Robert spent the three-day visit fishing while the women talked. Claudette's attention-span for conversation was short and she laughed out loud at nearly everything said.

Ilene told of her life. She had been placed in a dumpster at four months of age and also grew up in foster homes. She met her biological grandmother and a first cousin when she was eleven. Her cousin, Bonnie Whitehorse Weeks, was the one who gave Melinda Irene's phone number. Ilene said that their father had served time in prison for murder but had no other information about it.

The Klamath Tribal leader gave Claudette her tribal membership as a Klamath/Modoc Indian. She received many small items with the Tribal symbol and a DVD about the tribe. The elders made a special necklace for her. Ilene gave Claudette books on beading and some buffalo meat to take home and they parted with plans of getting together again.

As a member of the tribe, Claudette was part owner in the casino. She laughed when told that but didn't fully understand. Melinda took her to visit the gambling facility.

The Tribal newspaper featured a story on the long-awaited meeting and asked for information of other missing family members.

The Tribal newspaper didn't reach Larry Corville, in Bend, until July 30, 2007. Anxious to talk with his sister, he immediately called the number given to reach Claudette. He told Melinda the reason for Claudette's retardation was because as a baby she was held by the feet and slammed against a wall.

The last time Larry saw Claudette was when she was thirteen and she asked him for a piece of gum. He began making plans to bring the long-awaited gum when they met.

Sample Menu:
Sandwiches:
Tuna, Egg, or P&J
Soup:
Chicken Noodle or Tomato
Crackers
Three-bean Salad
Applesauce
Dessert

Still Simmering

He who aims for nothing, invariably hits it.

Hank Hanegraaff

"I haven't eaten in three days," a gentle voice on the phone sighed. "Isn't there anybody who can help me?" He softly pled.

The call came on a Saturday morning when Joyce Dart, long-time volunteer, and her husband, Ed, were delivering donations to the kitchen. Joyce explained the hours for the Soup Kitchen and read the list of other organizations that handed out food. None were open on Saturday.

"I'm hungry." The man stated, his voice filled with anxiety.

The Soup Kitchen rules stated that food was only given during serving hours. But once again, compassion superseded the rules. "Come on down. I'll find you something," Joyce promised.

"How do I get there?"

Joyce gave the directions then began searching the refrigerators and storage room for nutritious food that could be easily prepared and carried out.

Soon, a small-framed man arrived. A hint of curls, waved through his neatly trimmed, deep black hair. Sadness reflected in his brown eyes that sat behind dark-framed glasses. "I'm Ken," he extended his pale hand toward Ed, standing outside the Soup Kitchen door.

Ed quickly shook Ken's hand, explaining, "Well, you better talk to Joyce." Ed led him inside where Joyce was filling a plastic bag with a sandwich, an apple, some cookies and a fruit drink.

"This should help," Joyce patted his arm as she handed him the sack.

"Thank you." Ken timidly took the sack. "Is there something I can help with here?"

113

"We can always use volunteers to help clean up after our meals," Joyce quickly suggested.

"I'll help," he promised before he left with his food.

Joyce forgot about the young man until he appeared in the meal line Monday evening. "I can help tonight," he offered.

"Great. When you're finished eating talk to the lady in the red shirt," she said as she sat a piece of cake on his tray and pointed to Genna, who was picking up trays in the dining hall.

Ken finished his meal and eagerly began carrying heavy trays of plates through the sometimes congested doorway, around the ovens and to the dishwasher. I noticed his gentle manners in cleaning plates and wiping tables as I kept count of the guests that night.

"Is he a guest or a volunteer?" I asked Joyce when we finished serving. She told me of the phone call and how appreciative of the sandwich he was. He eagerly helped until the dining room was clean.

"Thank you for your help," Joyce said, smiling as Ken began to leave.

"I can come earlier," he suggested.

"That would be good. You can come in through the door over there." She pointed to the back of the kitchen.

Wednesday, Ken arrived to help set out towels, dishwasher trays and tubs of bleach water for wiping tables and trays. When everything was ready, he joined other cleanup volunteers to eat dinner before they began their work.

Friday, when Ken arrived I asked if he would tell me his story before it was time to serve. He agreed. We sat at an empty table while others worked on last minute preparations.

"I am not homeless," he was quick to explain. "I have been at times, but am not at this time."

"How come you had not eaten for several days when you called?" I asked, assuring him that he did not have to tell me anything he wasn't comfortable with.

"I have been out of work for two months with an injury." He raised his bandaged hand. "I have an ex-alcohol problem. It's better now but I did go on a drinking binge. When I went to the store to get beer, I saw the Soup Kitchen sign. That's when I went on the binge and when I woke up I was hungry." He shrugged his slender shoulders to note the irony. "I remembered the sign when I woke up."

He took a deep breath, slowly let it out and began his story. "I learned the street-life from my mother. She had a hard life, moved around a lot. I have been in many soup kitchens and shelters. I learned to use the system but I appreciate the system also." He pushed his glasses up his nose. "I was homeless in Colorado and came to Oregon in October 2006. It didn't take long to get a job at a food processing place. I asked them for help with my alcohol problem and they signed me up in a program. I start next week." A slight smile briefly lit his face.

"I haven't worked in two months and am behind on my rent. I start back to work next week and I'll have to leave here early to get to work, but I will be here," he firmly assured me before continuing. "I may get evicted though. It doesn't matter. I live simple. All I have is lounge chairs for sitting, one dish, one bowl, one cup, some silverware, a table and a bed. I'm always on the go and never accumulate much."

"What about relatives? Are there any in the area who might help?" I asked.

"No," he shook his head. "They are in Colorado. I haven't talked to my siblings in, uh, maybe four years. The less they know, the less I have to explain." He hesitated, wringing his hands. "I have missed a lot. I have a son in Colorado, and a granddaughter. I don't even know her name." His forehead furrowed. "That's stupid. I don't even know her name." A deep sigh escaped.

"How did you end up in Lebanon?" I hoped to find a brighter subject.

"I came because I had friends in Albany but then I stayed at a drug house in Lebanon until I found my own place." His sad eyes focused on me as if to be sure I understood. "I have dabbled in drugs but alcohol is the problem."

I thought of the old saying, "birds of a feather flock together." Or "Do not be misled: "Bad company corrupts good character."" (I Corinthians 15:33)

Ken's voice was barely audible at times as I strained to hear. "I've helped at other soup kitchens. I've eaten at soup kitchens when I didn't need to. I guess it was out of spite. Sometimes I'm embarrassed at who I am." He looked away. "Now I want to pay back and I'll be here to help as long as I live in the area."

He kept that promise, at least for awhile. Gradually, we saw less and less of him until he stopped coming. Maybe it was because he moved. No matter, I hoped he found whatever it was he was aiming for.

Sample Menu:
Clam Chowder
Bread Bowl
Corn
Green Salad
Peaches
Dessert

Spreading Encouragement

I like living. I have sometimes been wildly, despairingly, acutely miserable, racked with sorrow, but through it all I still know quite certainly that just to be alive is a grand thing.

Agatha Christie

"No drugs on you or in you," read the bold sign hung on the door of Ron's small trailer house nestled in the trees next to an historic home. For 13 years Ron welcomed anyone who wanted to stop for a visit and occasionally spend the night out of the cold but when he put the sign up, the visits slowed. "Doug comes over to watch wrestling," he explained, elbowing the younger man sitting next to him.

"That's okay," Ron shrugged his narrow shoulders and leaned back in the hard, metal chair at the Soup Kitchen. "I got ripped off a lot. I've lost $4,000 or $5,000 over the years. I still keep trying to pull them out of that life." Ron knew what it was like to be homeless and he opened his doors despite the inevitable loss of TVs, VCRs, tools and more. "It didn't matter if they were high-life, low-life or mid-life, I could communicate with them. I wanted to let them know someone cared." His thick, black hair contrasted his weathered face creased with years of hard living. He was probably a dashing man in his youth.

"I have lived in my car at River Park and in homeless shelters in Albany and Corvallis. In Corvallis, they made me assistant manager at the shelter. One time I met a kid at the Big O Restaurant and visited with him. Later my boss sent me to the hospital to pick up a homeless guy with burns from a can explosion. It was him. That kid stuck to me like glue. I decided to get my life together and help others get out of their mess.

117

"While I was helping them out, I introduced Frank to Mary. I was pushing them to get jobs and do the right thing with their lives. They stopped drinking and got their lives together. They have been married eight years and are doing good.

"I helped a lot of kids the best I could. One girl told me she was going to run away from home. She couldn't get along with her mom. "Look at yourself," I said, "and your mom. She doesn't want you to turn out like herself. The best thing you can do is go back, throw your arms around your mom and say, "I love you. I know what you are trying to do." She took my advice." His dark brown eyes shined with pride. "When I met her parents, she introduced me as her town Dad.

"Some can't be helped. I know this lady. Her son lives with her. He had a job at the mill for two weeks and lost it. He spent everything he made on booze. He can't keep a job because of his drinking."

Ron shook a long, thin finger toward another regular guest carrying his tray to an adjacent table. "Hey! Did you see that game last night?" he smiled broadly.

"They only won by one run," the man quickly shot back, laughing.

Ron looked around the dining hall and waved to a couple just arriving, then turned his head back toward me. "I have no food or money half the time. Arnie introduced me to the Soup Kitchen." He motioned toward a husky man sitting at another table. "I've been coming ever since. I can't cook. Cooked toast twice. There was so much smoke, the neighbors called the fire department both times." A deep laugh rumbled from behind his crooked smile.

"I have gotten to know a lot of people here. I like to stick by those who are down. Help them keep their head out of the gutter. I work with them, encourage them."

Ron sipped his cooling coffee. "I think of these kids as my own." His bright eyes narrowed. "I've lost two girls and one boy to murder; all within six months. I lost seven friends and relatives, including my dad, in that time."

Ron's dad was mayor of Sodaville. At that time, Ron volunteered to work for the small town. He checked on wells, pressure gauges, well-ducts and waterlines to the fire hydrants. He enjoyed the work and helping the community.

Being politically active was a hobby for him. "I wanted to be the people's voice, so I ran for Lebanon's mayor in 2004. Those running were campaigning for things we didn't need. I got 4 percent of the vote. That's more than Ross Perot got for president. It was the first time Lebanon had three candidates." He laughed. "I fought last year to get the new court house, library and police station in Lebanon." He hesitated while the edges of his mouth pushed his cheeks upward, deepening the furrows around his protruding check bones. "It passed," he firmly stated, slamming his hand on the table.

Campaigning in politics wasn't his only battle. "I've been fighting for 19 months to get disability. I have syncope E syndrome*, which means stress or anxiety causes me to go paralyzed for three to five minutes." He shook his head. "I still haven't seen any money even though they said I was disabled."

Ron lowered his deep voice, "I have helped the cops a few times. If they are looking for someone, I can tell them where he is. I bought a chainsaw from some crooks for the police. That broke open a sale-of-stolen-property deal in Eugene. When I worked for Pinkerton guarding Craig's, a crook asked me to turn my back for 15 minutes so he could rip them off. I wouldn't do it." He raised his voice a little.

A middle-aged woman slid her arm across Ron's back, her small hand gently squeezed his shoulder. "I'm going to miss you. You've been a good friend."

His rough hand patted hers. "You have, too."

She smiled and gave him a hug.

Ron was leaving Lebanon and this was his last meal at the Soup Kitchen. The charming gentleman who befriended many was starting a new chapter in his life. He purchased a train ticket to Missouri to live near the son he never really knew.

"The last time I saw my son was in 1992 when he was 20 years old. He stayed a month with me and left. We lost contact until this year." A sigh slipped from deep within as he drifted away in thought. Taking a shallow breath, he continued, "I found him on the computer. There were several people with his name. I called the police department in the town listed by each name to ask about him. I found him with the second call." He started to pick up his coffee cup, hesitated and shook his head, "My son don't know me yet. We have been communicating for eight months, but he don't know his dad." Sorrow slipped into his usually bright eyes as he sat quietly.

How ironic that so many young people called him "Dad," yet his own son never saw the traits that earned him that endearment. Maybe the reconciliation would heal the 35 years of separation.

Ron's deep voice rang with excitement and hope as he repeated his train ride schedule to his son's home. He knew the harshness found in living but learned to cherish life. He wanted others, especially young people, to make it a grand thing.

Sample Menu:
Turkey
Stuffing
Mashed Potatoes and Gravy
Fruit Salad
Green Salad
Applesauce
Blueberry Cobbler
Whipped Cream

Assortment of Flavors

When you love people, you see all the good in them, all the Christ in them. God sees Christ, His son, in us. And so we should see Christ in others, and nothing else, and love them.

Dorothy Day, Founder of Catholic Workers

People come to the Soup Kitchen with their own stories of the paths that lead them to this place in their lives.

Arnie's mother and step-father handed him over to the justice system to be a ward of the court when he was 16 years old. They did not want to deal with him any longer. Arnie was a good kid. He wasn't in any trouble. He wasn't rebellious. He had epilepsy.

The time and expense of his condition left his mother worn out and the epileptic seizures prevented Arnie from living on his own. The court placed him in a group home in Portland. His mother seldom visited, but his sister, Pauline, was faithful in taking him for weekend outings.

This was not the first time Arnie felt abandoned by a parent. His father left the family when Arnie was five years old, leaving him without a male figure to look up to. But like many five-year-olds Arnie had heroes. His were Roy Rogers and Dale Evans and they were going to be the Grand Marshals at a parade in Eugene. Arnie was filled with excitement when his mother took him to see the parade. But Arnie didn't watch the parade. Before it started, the confident five-year-old boldly walked up to Roy Rogers and asked if he could ride Trigger, Rogers' horse. Rogers sat the excited little boy in the saddle and they rode through the parade together.

Along the route, Arnie asked Roy if he would be his daddy, since he no longer had one. "From now on, consider yourself an adopted son," Roy told him. Arnie's hero was now his surrogate father and they kept in touch through letters. Arnie moved many times over the years and eventually lost contact with his hero. He collected Roy Rogers memorabilia, each piece held a link to his cherished memories. His voice struggled to contain his excitement when telling others of his story.

One night at the Soup Kitchen, Arnie received a special gift from Joyce, a volunteer. She had returned from one of her extended trips RVing around the country and brought Arnie an 8"x10" color photograph of Roy Rogers, Dale Evans and their son, Roy Jr. Arnie was breathless when he read the note and signature on the picture. Roy Jr. signed the picture, 'Happy Trails, to my son,' and added his father's name. Arnie treasures that photograph and his friendship with Joyce for remembering him on her travels.

The Soup Kitchen was a second family for Arnie. He made many friends over the years. "I don't have to eat here," he told me one night. "I live with my niece and this gives her a break from cooking for me." Leaning closer, he quietly continued, "Besides, I like seeing my friends here."

Arnie's hardy laugh could be heard each night as he joked with many of the guests. "Hi, Sweetheart," he greeted me as he came through the food line.

One evening I handed him an empty plate. "You didn't want anything tonight did you?"

He reached for the plate. "Hey," he hollered. "You'd better stop that or I'll give you a kiss." A kiss was his usual threat when someone teased him. We chuckled as I placed meat, vegetables and salad on a plate and handed it to him.

He joked with many long-time friends, but also showed his concern for others. Majel, a volunteer who took the nightly count, fell at her home and wasn't at the Soup Kitchen for a couple of weeks. I filled in for her and explained her condition as people asked for her each night.

Arnie's chest puffed with pride as he announced that he would get her a get-well card for everyone to sign. Sure enough, Arnie brought a card. Following the meal, Arnie proudly gave the signature-covered card to another volunteer to take to Majel.

Arnie often stayed through the serving-hour and if help was needed he swept or mopped floors. Not leaving until closing also gave him the opportunity to catch a ride home with someone.

Another regular who often helped pick up trays and dirty plates was Doug. His shiny, light brown hair hung in a ponytail down his back. He had a mustache and sometimes a fu-man-chu, other times he had a beard. However he came, he was a welcomed sight.

One day, sitting across the table at the Soup Kitchen, Doug confided in me, "I had a job and a home. I wanted to make some things right and went to jail for it. While I was in jail my roommate sold all of my stuff." He shrugged his narrow shoulders. "I just learned to be a survivor." Homeless since 2002, Doug camped in a tent. "Most people don't want to be homeless." He glanced across the table at a thin man in his forties, "John helped me at first. I learned when you are camping you need to be firm and take a stand to protect your stuff or others will trash it or take it." He finished a glass of milk.

"I have no relatives and the system is not set up for single men. Living outdoors, I do get sick a lot." He shook his head as if to shake off the negative words. "But I have a friend who lets me cook and shower at his house. I know I will get out of this someday." His soothing voice held optimism for his future. "We are on God's time not ours."

I glanced at the ring on his hand inscribed "Faith=Trust." "So are you religious?"

"I'm spiritual, not religious. Religion argues over differences and says that someone is always worse. I don't like that."

One reason Doug was homeless was because he injured his back and couldn't work and couldn't afford the needed surgery. Without the surgery, he couldn't get a job. Without a job, he couldn't save money for the surgery. The perpetual cycle familiar with many caught in need. But Doug kept a positive attitude.

He pulled a San Francisco 49ers stocking cap over his ears and picked up his plate, along with several others on the table. "The Soup Kitchen gives me sleeping bags and tents and feeds me three days a week. That's why I don't mind helping."

Doug also helped Genna by accompanying her to meetings to establish a homeless shelter. He used his experience to testify for the need.

Johnny was another guest who pitched in to help, even cooking. Besides the Soup Kitchen, he also worked at the Lord's Storehouse. But seizures plagued his health and limited his ability to volunteer regularly at either. He lived in a one-bedroom building and let families who needed help live with him.

After years of coming to the Soup Kitchen, he confided in Joe, a volunteer, that he would like to go to church but didn't knout how to find one. His fear of church was keeping him away. Joe invited him to a Bible study group at his home. Johnny accepted the offer and his regular attendance at the Bible study inspired his wife to return to the church she grew up in.

One visitor, who ate and stayed to mop the floor, said he did it "because Jesus is coming." That was a great reason.

Many guests came and never washed a plate or mopped the floor, but they helped the spirits of the volunteers with their appreciation. One of those was Jess. "It helps to get a hot meal. I don't cook. Don't know what to fix," he told me. He was a veteran who spent six months in a VA hospital. He received disability benefits in 1982. "Life is easier on disability. I don't have the stress of being around people. I am thankful for what I have, but I am not satisfied with my life. I keep it simple. I go to church every Sunday. I don't prowl around." Deep brown eyes and a trimmed mustache added color to his bald head and round, rugged face. "The Soup Kitchen has affected me in a positive way. I'm glad it is here."

Dave, a retiree from Willamette Industries, smiled and added, "I just want a good meal."

Cliff seldom thanked anyone for a meal but probably never thought about it. Coming to the Soup Kitchen was routine. He came near the end of serving time and quietly ate while volunteers cleaned up around him. If he was late, a container was filled and he ate on the bench in front of the building. He lived out of his car but had a tent for occasional camping. He often used the restroom for a sponge bath and to change clothes, leaving a wet mess for others to clean up. For a time, he borrowed the phone to schedule the next day's yard-work for other people.

Using the phone, which only makes local calls, has been an asset for others. Carol, a woman in her fifties with thin, brown hair made a phone call after most meals. I always assumed it was for a ride home. One night she came in with red eyes and in a shaky voice asked Kandi, the manager, if she could go into the sanctuary to pray. I finished cutting additional desert to serve, then told Kandi, "I'll see if she is okay." Carol was standing near the heater in the dining hall when I gently touched her arm to get her attention. "Would you like someone to pray with you?" I asked.

Her large, brown eyes fixed on me a moment before she answered, "I already did." She hesitated, still studying me. "Anyway, Genna's not here." I was familiar with the lady but Genna was her confidant. I wasn't insulted by her reluctance to share with me.

"Are you okay now?" I asked.

Tears formed in her eyes. "It's hard to lose three parents in two years (one was a step-parent)," she mumbled. "I miss them so much."

I took her hand, "I'm so sorry."

"They died in August and October." She wiped stringy, gray hair from her tanned face. "We were close." She stared at the floor as if lost in thought. A forced smile revealed missing front teeth. She assured me, "I feel better already."

Each of these stories shows the vulnerable humanity in all of us. By listening with an open heart I have tried to learn to see the good which every soul possesses, somewhere, sometime. When we see the Christ in others we cannot keep from loving them as we were commanded by Jesus in John 13:34 "Just as I have loved you, you should love each other."

Sample Menu:
Lasagna
French Bread
Carrots
Green Salad
Mixed Fruit
Dessert

Nurtures Needs

"Good works are links that form a chain of love."
Mother Teresa

Thanksgiving and Christmas are times for being thankful and giving. That was the time of year Patty and her daughter, Cindy, began volunteering at the Soup Kitchen. Both thankfulness and giving was a large part of Patty's life.

She had recently moved to Lebanon to help Cindy with daily tasks that her fibromyalgia-stricken body could no longer do. The work at the Soup Kitchen proved too taxing and soon Cindy stopped coming.

Patty's devotion continued. "I felt this was a place where I could pour out my love for others while serving them. There was a lot to learn and many wonderful people to work with. My life had a new spark that filled me with joy." That spark also filled her brown eyes as she talked.

"Working here touched a part of me I never knew was there. It changed my opinion of people and it wasn't long before I realized I was the one being loved and encouraged by the guests. Smiles, gratitude, appreciation, laughter and words of welcome flowed from people who had so little, not even a winter coat. My heart held pangs of guilt because I had two." Her radiant smile faded.

"I asked the Lord to show me how to be His servant and for His help in touching those in need. My eyes, heart, mind and spirit were opened. My new journey had begun." Her smile returned and her narrow face held a peace that reflected the confidence of her faith. "At the Soup Kitchen I was guided to individuals. In a quiet voice, away from listening ears I would ask, 'If someone could help you get something you need, what would it be?'"

Some of the replies were:

"Pay for my medication. I have a prescription and I can't get it filled."

"I had a bike to get around, but it was stolen."

"My duffel bag is so worn that I have it taped up so that my clothes don't fall out."

"Help me get my paperwork done so I can get benefits for my medical problems and my military service."

"A camp stove."

"I live out of my van and it needs repair work."

"I need food at our campsite for the days when the kitchen isn't open."

"I need blankets and a tent."

"I need heavy, thick socks."

"I need boots."

"A new backpack, mine is ripping apart."

"I need a winter coat and warm hat for my baby."

The answers were simple, honest needs, but many people found it hard to voice what they could use. Patty sighed after recalling the list. "The integrity in their answers was pure and they had no greed. I was left in a state of wonder."

Several people only wanted help getting their identification papers, copies of their birth certificates, social security cards, or state ID cards; things lost long ago when food, shelter and clothes became a priority.

"I helped one man with the paperwork he needed to get his social security card and county ID. Then I connected him with a representative at the Veteran's office. He was able to get disability benefit. He started improving his life and is doing well now." Patty paused, "He came back to try to help others in similar situations."

Another of those stories was that of Bulldog. In the busy dining hall one night he called to Patty, "Hey, Sister!" She remembered her first reaction.

"Even before I turned toward the voice, my heart was lifted by the Holy Spirit," Patty said. "I looked to see a man with a full, long salt-and pepper-beard. He was not very tall, maybe five-five. He wore a well-aged leather jacket and worn, baggy blue jeans. His calloused hands showed years of rough use, along with camp dirt, as they fumbled with a knitted wool hat. His blue eyes held a sparkle and glistened with joyful laughter and delight. His hair was shoulder length, slightly thinning on the top and held hints of silver. It was apparent by his flattened nose and scars across his forehead that he had survived some traumatic event. His smile stunned me. It was the softening factor of his weathered face."

Bulldog's full lips held his toothless secret until he spoke. "Sister, I just want to thank you for all you do. I really appreciate it. God bless you."

Patty instantly gave him a big hug. From then on, she held a sandwich aside and watched for him. She sidled up to him, slid the sandwich in his pocket and whispered, "For later."

"I know just the person who needs this," was his usual answer. "Thank you, Sister."

As time passed Patty learned that Bulldog's weakness was in the bending of his elbow with a can of beer firmly secured in his hand. "His drinking never detracted from his courteousness, kindness and gentlemanly manner." She described the man who was probably in his late fifties. "Whether drunk or sober there was always the heartfelt, "Thank you, Sister." And he was always willing to share his meager check, and his buddies knew it."

Patty asked Bulldog the question she asked many others, "What would you like the most for someone to help you with?" His response was simple: an identification card. His birth certificate, social security card and medical coverage card had been lost. Without one, he couldn't get the others which left him with no way to begin the process.

Sitting in the noise-filled dining area, Bulldog told Patty his birth information. She wrote a letter requesting a copy of his birth certificate and he signed it.

A week later, a letter arrived explaining that no birth certificate could be issued because the person in question had died many years ago. "I was shocked and anxious to show the letter to Bulldog," Patty laughed while recalling the letter.

"Well, Sister, you can see that I am not dead, that's for sure." Bulldog nonchalantly smiled. "I was born a twin and my brother is the one who died on the date given in the letter."

Patty couldn't wait until the next morning so she could call The Department of Records in Salem. This information provided the resolution to confusing problems and errors that had long plagued the department. The records showed that it was Darold (Bulldog) who had died instead of his twin, Gerald.

With the mystery cleared up, Bulldog soon had his birth certificate. "His rough hands caressed the document while he studied it, as though it was a map to untold riches." Joy flowed in Patty's soft voice. "In a way, it was. It showed who he was. It was his heart's desire to have the document that society deemed a requirement in validating his existence. His moistened eyes radiated with joy and pride."

Patty never seemed to grow tired of helping the needy. Her actions followed the words in Galatians 6:9-10, "Let us not become weary in doing good, for at proper time we will reap a harvest if we do not give up. Therefore, as we have opportunity, let us do good to all people."

Patty designed and printed 2007 calendars which were sold as a benefit for the Soup Kitchen. Each month had a photograph of volunteers or guests.

She visited the Soup Kitchen regularly to help with special events, like filling baskets for Easter, Christmas or Halloween. And with pen and paper in hand, she continued roaming through the dining room and asked, "If someone could help you get something you need, what would it be?" She returned a few days later with the requested gloves, socks or dog food.

The Lord provided for Bulldog and the others Patty spoke with. Patty's heart poured out for all of them as she fondly remembered them. "I love each and every one and cherish my time spent with them. I received more than I could give back. They gave me hugs, smiles, laughter, love and special joy."

Connected by a chain of love, people gave without knowing who their gifts were going to.

Sample Menu:

Sauerkraut and Hot Dogs

Potato Salad

Veggie basket with dip

Pears

Dessert

More Than Food

"Kind words can be short and easy to speak, but their echoes are truly endless."

Mother Teresa

Splinters of ice scattered as the sharp ax chipped away the freshly frozen water, exposing the flowing river beneath. The ice had grown thick during the cold spell that had settled in the valley but the cattle needed water. The ice hole along the bank had to be re-opened each morning.

After widening the hole, I secured the ax on the fender of the tractor. The drive through the field took me past the cattle eating hay on the snow-covered ground. I carefully scanned the herd for sick or injured animals and watched the swelling udders for signs of impending birth. The cows near calving needed to be watched closely. Sub-zero temperatures could be fatal to a newborn. Many calves had to be laid by the woodstove in the house to dry and warm before returning to their mothers.

Like my experience of tending cattle in Eastern Oregon, Jesus' disciple, Peter, understood that feeding encompassed the whole care of the animal. When Jesus said "feed my sheep," he knew Jesus meant more than providing food. He also knew that Jesus was not referring to a flock of sheep, but to the people Peter ministered to.

The Soup Kitchen's purpose was to provide food, but the volunteers soon learned that some people coming needed more than a hot meal.

"Where can I get food the rest of the week?" A mother with three little girls asked one of the volunteers. "I have a job interview, but I don't have money for gas so I can get there. Can anyone help me?" a young man wondered. "My husband just threw us out. Is there somewhere to sleep tonight?" pleaded a young woman holding a baby.

These types of questions were asked regularly during meals. There were places that could help, if those in need knew where to go. Marcy printed a paper showing when and where to attain food and posted it at the Soup Kitchen entrance. She found an agency that would help with housing for one night and another that would help with gas. For someone seeking aid these resources needed to be easier to find. This information should be available in one location.

The Soup Kitchen board discussed this need and asked an established facility in Corvallis for help. An experienced counselor trained a group of volunteers to operate a referral center. The volunteers were only to dispense information and not offer counseling.

The church provided a small room at the front of the building for an office, which would be opened four afternoons a week. The office opened onto the sidewalk that went to the Soup Kitchen, making it easily accessible.

When the Lebanon Basic Services Center opened in the fall of 1991, I spent four hours, one afternoon a week, volunteering to answer the phone and talk with people who stopped in. An old wooden desk and swivel chair sat near the door with a long table beside it. Two metal folding chairs were in front of the table. The desk held the phone numbers and information for where and when nearly every kind of help was available.

The volunteers' job was to refer people to someone trained to handle their situation and it didn't take long to steer them on their way with the proper information. Many of the phone calls were completed in minutes and the occasional visitor received their information quickly and left. Most of my time was spent reading or writing letters to friends during the long silence between client interactions. Some afternoons could be on the edge of boring. Some weren't.

One quiet day my reading was interrupted when a dark-haired young woman, breathing heavily came through the door quickly and carefully closed it behind her. Her tanned face was hardened by firm-set jaws and narrow eyes that were red and puffy.

"May I help you?" I asked.

Her head jerked up as if startled. "Ya. I just need to set down a few minutes." She pulled a folding chair to the corner of the room and sat down. "My boyfriend is looking for me." She explained between breaths. "That SOB has gone too far too many times. I am leaving him this time." She watched the door. "He thinks I'll go back if he can find me."

I noticed the red mark beginning to swell on her check. "I'll call the police for you," I reached for the phone.

"No," she snapped. "I'll be fine. He doesn't know where I am."

"You need to report this to the police, especially if it has happened before."

"He thinks he can treat me like this but I'll show him." Anger raged in her eyes. "I can walk away." She stood and walked across the room, pounding her palm with her other hand. "I'm not going to take this. I am <u>not</u> going back."

"Where will you go?" I asked, dialing the police.

"Anywhere except with him." Her deep voice rang. "He treats me like dirt. He isn't going to get away with it this time."

"An officer is on his way. At least you can talk to him." I said, hanging up the phone.

Her slim frame sank onto the cold chair and she tipped her head back against the wall. "Why haven't I done this before?" She sighed.

"At least you are doing…" I was interrupted by the door swinging open. *That was quick,* I thought, expecting the officer. My heart sank as I watched a burly man fill the doorway. His steely eyes fixed on the young woman who cowered in the corner.

"Let's go." His harsh voice demanded.

She looked at the floor, rubbing her hands on her arms.

"I don't think she wants to go with you." I stood behind my desk and held my voice as steady as I could. He slowly turned toward me, only the desk between us. I held my breath and watched his thick, muscled arm bulge as he raised a fist in warning.

"This is none of your business." His cold, hard eyes pierced through me. He turned back to the trembling woman and barked, "Let's go." He grabbed her arm and yanked her off the chair. Her chin brushed her chest, with her eyes fixed on her feet as he dragged her out the door, slamming it behind them.

I watched out the window as he led her toward an old, beat-up sedan. A police car pulled to the curb in front of the car. After a brief exchange of words the police officer handcuffed the man and led him to the patrol car. The man stopped beside the patrol car and stared back at the crying young woman. She still stood beside the sedan where he pushed her when the policeman arrived. Her eyes briefly looked toward him and she turned to walk away.

Remembering those cold eyes, I felt a quiver run down my back. I slumped in my chair and took a long, deep breath. I wondered if she would find the strength to keep walking. The strength she briefly displayed when he was not present.

On another slow afternoon, I hung up the phone after keeping the caller on the line as long as I could. While I recorded the call in the record book, a man in his twenties came in. I looked up to greet him and was met by dark eyes full of rage.

"If you don't give me a reason to live, I will kill myself right here," his rough voice barked, raising a five-inch knife in his clutched fist to emphasize his threat.

A gasp escaped my lips as my heart began to pound. My mind raced through my training for the proper response but only remembered the instructor's emphatic words, "You will never have to deal with suicide threats, so we don't need to cover it."

"Why don't you sit down?" I heard words spill from my mouth. I inhaled a slow, deep breath and thought of the words of Colossians 4:6, "Let your conversation be gracious and effective so that you will have the right answer for everyone." *God, give me the words to say.* I eased the air from my lungs and my heart steadied its beats. "Why would you want to kill yourself?" I asked.

"I'm going to court tomorrow. I'll go to jail. I'll lose my job. I've messed everything up!" Moisture filled his eyes, melting the rage as he continued to outline his desperate situation with fear for his future.

As he named each problem, I could feel the weight of confusion growing heavier. Wide scars covered both wrists of his muscular arms, evidence that he was capable of carrying out his threat.

"What if we just talked about one problem for now?" I asked. "What are you going to court for?"

He explained how he hung out with the wrong crowd and had gone along with a burglary.

"If you go to your hearing tomorrow, what is the worst that could happen?"

He wiped a tear from his cheek. His forehead wrinkled as he narrowed his eyes in a questioning gaze. "I could go to jail," he firmly responded.

"If you go to jail, what is the worse that could happen?"

The next 90 minutes were a haze of what ifs. His voice became calm as we talked about how to deal with each scenario in a positive way. We broke each problem apart and looked at the pieces.

He folded the knife and slid it into his pocket. His stiff body relaxed enough to laugh a couple of times when we talked of more light-hearted subjects.

"Would you talk to a pastor?" I suggested. The angry person who threatened suicide was transformed to a relaxed man envisioning hope, but I believed he needed continual help.

"I'm Catholic."

"I can call the Catholic Church and see if the priest could talk with you now," I offered while looking up the phone number.

"Ok," he mumbled.

I hung up the phone and looked him in the eyes. "The priest is expecting you in about eight minutes. It's not far and that's enough time to walk there."

He stood and wiped more tears from his eyes. "I can't thank you enough. You showed me a new way of looking at things."

I gripped his hand in a firm shake. "You'll be fine. Just deal with one problem at a time," I encouraged as he left.

I didn't hear from the priest in the next 15 minutes so I knew the young man arrived at his office. That would be the last time I saw him, I thought, hoping he found a way to improve his situation.

A few weeks later, I was surprised when I found him scraping plates at the Soup Kitchen. The sad eyes had become bright and a smile highlighted his rugged face. He shared his carefully written poems about his dark days and how he found joy. Others at the Soup Kitchen could relate to his personal struggle. He helped at the Soup Kitchen for several months before moving on in his life.

The Basic Services reminded me of ranching. Whether it was chipping away at problems or protecting from predators, each was a place of caring for needs. The Basic Services helped improve some people's lives, some it didn't and others we would never know. Each received the information needed and chose how to use it. The Basic Services Center provided more than a hot meal could fill.

Sample Menu:
Tuna Casserole
Potato Wedges
Green Salad
Bread
Fruit Jell-O
Dessert

Doubles the Recipe

God is in the Details.

Ludwig Mies Van Der Rohe

"Coming through," hollered a volunteer in the busy kitchen as she slid past other volunteers in the narrow space encircling the stove at the center of the room. A countertop ran along the back wall, only three and a half feet from the front of the ovens. A sink and more countertop at each end of the room were five feet from the sides of the stove but shelves along the stove narrowed the distance to three and a half feet. The serving counter was three and a half feet from the back of the stove.

With a cook and two or three volunteers working to prepare the evening meal, the area was cramped. If a door or drawer needed to be opened to retrieve utensils, pans or ingredients, all movement came to a halt until it could be closed again. When the oven door was open while cooking, the heat instantly filled the tight quarters, creating a sauna in the hot summer months.

Cabinets above the counters provided area for essentials to be kept but the storage room was inconveniently located in another part of the church. The kitchen, built in 1949, became an obstacle for the efficiency of preparing meals. A larger more effective kitchen became a dream of many who worked in the cramped quarters.

In April 1998, Frank Crowley, a cook, presented the Soup Kitchen board with an idea for a 21x25 foot addition that would include two showers and a laundry. Crowley, Mike Wells and Terry Williams solicited materials for the addition and talked with a representative from the Willamette Valley Home Builders Association (WVHBA). In 1999, they worked with an architect to present the board with a revised proposal. Building and maintaining showers and a laundry were not feasible with the area and the regulations they had to work with. The addition plan was changed to 20x30 feet with ample room for cooking and storage.

Crowley's optimism and hard work were cut short by the lack of funds to instigate the project. Unfortunately, Crowley passed away before his dream could become a reality. However, soon after his death an estate gift breathed new hope into the building addition.

Dora Kellenberger Hall developed an interest in the Soup Kitchen from reports Bev Copeland regularly gave at their church. Dora was a prominent Lebanon resident and along with her first husband operated an appliance store for many years. Dora passed away in 2002 leaving $7.4 million to several charitable organizations, of which a small amount was given to the First Christian Church with the designation that it be used to support the Soup Kitchen or like organizations to help the homeless and hungry.

The estate money was a boost but would not be enough to complete the construction. Joyce Dart, co-coordinator of the Soup Kitchen, saw an article in the Democrat-Herald and Corvallis Gazette-Times asking for requests for their featured "Nonprofit Wishes." She sent the Soup Kitchen's wish. Part of the letter read, "At this point our **WISH** is that an architect would draw up the plans and a contractor would give a bid" to have the kitchen enlarged. She requested funds to match the Kellenberger gift, explaining that the enlargement would make the kitchen more convenient, more cost efficient and a safer place to work.

Don Gibson and Elmer Breckel, members of the First Christian Church, drew a rough sketch for the addition plans, presented them to the Soup Kitchen Board December 4, 2002, and waited for an architect to review them.

On Christmas day, an article in the newspaper featured the Soup Kitchen and its wish. Walt Rebmann, owner of Buck Construction and a member of the board of directors for the WVHBA, read the article. "I never read those things. I just happened to see it," he smiled, recalling how he became involved. He remembered Frank Crowley's idea presented to WVHBA several years before. "I had an idea of what they wanted to do, what's there and how it can work," Walt told me one afternoon while we visited at the Soup Kitchen. "I called Joyce and attended the Soup Kitchen Board meeting."

By late January 2003, Walt became the general contractor to oversee the project and keep the costs as low as possible. He proposed the plans to the WVHBA as one of their community projects. "We call them our "warm and fuzzy" projects," Walt laughed. "We want to help the community in some way. Their philosophy is like mine; what is our job on Earth? It is to help people."

Walt was also a member of Linn County Affordable Housing, who helped him locate a Eugene architect, Sarah Bergsund, to design a plan. She massaged Don and Elmer's sketch and changes were made to lower costs and to meet building codes. In three months, the plans were complete and taken to the

Lebanon Planning Department. "People there were helpful in getting the plans approved," Walt praised the ones who guided him in the approval process.

One of the obstacles was the Soup Kitchen Board's desire to have an electrical meter in the addition, separate from the one for the church. According to regulations, two meters could not be placed in the same building. Without the Soup Kitchen's own meter, the plans for the addition couldn't be approved. However, the existing meter was two phase and the dishwasher needed three phase. A second meter needed to be installed for the three phase. The dishwasher was essential for operation so the second meter was allowed and the construction approved.

While Walt contacted sub-contractors, Joyce Dart looked for additional money to help with the project. She knew funds were available if someone could write a grant to apply for them. She was lamenting the problem one day during an eye exam. Her doctor, Dr. Dennis Pearson, quickly volunteered his years of experience as a grant writer. "Thank you, Lord," Joyce shouted. Dr. Pearson, Doug Parker and Terry Lewis wrote grants to various organizations.

Eventually, grants for the renovation were awarded from Weyerhaeuser Company Foundation, Oregon Community Foundation, Meyer Memorial Trust, Ford Family Foundation and Collins Foundation. These grants, along with the money from the Kellenberger estate, enabled the project to proceed. Additional grants were later written to help with the remaining costs.

Don Gibson, a member of the Soup Kitchen board, explained applying for grant money as a way to invest what was given them, like the story in Matthew 25:14-18. A master entrusted three servants with different amounts of money. Two invested theirs and doubled the amount, while the third buried his and received nothing in the end. God provided the Soup Kitchen with the estate money and they used it as a foundation to apply for grants. Their efforts were honored with the necessary funds.

Construction began in late 2004. Framing the walls was done largely by Don, Elmer and Walt. The electrical, plumbing and sheetrock were completed by sub-contractors who Walt previously worked with. "We built trust by years of treating each other fairly," he said with confidence in the sub-contractors.

One of Walt's previous contracts was with the Lebanon Senior Center. When the Senior Center moved from their small building on Park Street to the old Lebanon Middle School building, they replaced the dishwasher in the building with their nearly new one. The city council, who owned the building, voted unanimously to donate the $6000 dishwasher from the old school building to the Soup Kitchen. With minor repairs, it was like new and a great asset to the operation of the kitchen.

The 53-year-old building presented some problems. One was not having information on the original construction and therefore, not knowing what kind of concrete was beneath the church wall being removed. "Without knowing what type was there, we didn't know what needed to be done," Walt explained. "We had to learn and design as we went."

Another problem was the aging brick on the outside of the building. Plans were to match the new wall to the existing one but brick patterns and colors change over the years and finding a similar brick created a concern. Walt began his search, locating an exact match at the first location where he looked.

"There were problems but never so big they couldn't be solved," Walt said while finishing a bowl of blueberries. "It took planning but everything worked out well, considering it was decided by a committee, like coordinating the color of tiles and walls."

Walt's efforts saved the Soup Kitchen between $20,000 and $25,000 through donated labor and supplies. "It is easier to work when you like what you do and who you work with. It was fun." But he won't take the credit for the completion of the worthy project. "It was a group effort. They all did their part." This was his last job before retiring.

Don also donated hours of his time in the construction. "The project was well worth my time. I was retired and had time on my hands. It was a constructive way to use my time." He laughed while recalling the work. "There were times, like painting, others would help and it would be fun, more like play than work. Different people came to do different jobs but it all came out in the end. It is something that will still give after I'm gone."

The volunteers worked on the project when they were available from their jobs, making the progress slow. The job took approximately four months to complete. The circumstances that brought it all together followed God's timing. "Many are the plans in a man's heart, but it is the Lord's purpose that prevails." (Proverbs 19:21)

Serving meals never stopped during construction. When the kitchen couldn't be used, sack lunches were handed out at the door.

The 720-square-foot addition doubled the size of the kitchen. The 24- by 30-foot area included additional sinks and counter space for preparation, along with a pantry, a commercial dishwasher and space for freezers and refrigerators.

The design for the addition did not include a walk-in freezer but one was later added, replacing five upright freezers. The walk-in was well worth the cost. "It had one compressor, instead of five," Elmer said. "It saves energy and I don't have to be down here all the time fixing it." He referred to the problems always developing with the uprights.

A cement slab was poured in front of the new addition and the area covered with a roof, providing shelter for diners waiting in line. A bench was added against the building for limited seating.

Several months after completion, on July 7, 2005, a ribbon-cutting ceremony and open house were held to celebrate. Approximately 70 people gathered in the parking lot in front of the new building to thank God for all those who made it possible.

Dedicated in memory of Frank Crowley, a plaque read, "for his vision many years ago of this project." Frank was well known for his loyalty and hard work at the Soup Kitchen. Also honored were Elmer Breckel, Don Gibson and Walt Rebmann for their hours of labor. Joyce Dart and Melva Hessevick were recognized for their dedication of 16 years as the Soup Kitchen coordinator and treasurer. Manager Kandi Gregory was presented with a one-year award, while Merthal Settlemier, who was celebrating her 88th birthday, was recognized not only for her contributions but for her presence as well.

A banner listing all the businesses who donated time, supplies or money was printed and hung on the fence along the gas station property.

People marveling at the spacious new kitchen couldn't imagine how the volunteers ever worked in the cramped area of the old one. But they did, for 16 years and did a terrific job. After years of man's planning, God brought the details together.

Sample Menu:
Hamburger Soup with Rice
Bread
Green Salad
Pudding
Dessert

Courtesy of Soup Kitchen
Don painting the new addition.

Dishes Up Hospitality

Hospitality is one form of worship.

The Talmud

The sun's rays reflected off the red brick side of the church, heating the area in front of the Soup Kitchen doors where a group of hungry diners waited for the evening meal. A young woman in an oversized white shirt and spandex shorts walked ahead of me toward those gathered.

"Debbie," called a petite woman as she emerged from the smoking area behind the large blue dumpster to the right of the kitchen entry. "I haven't seen you in along time."

"Rachel," the young woman responded with surprise and joy. The two embraced in a caring hug.

I continued toward the entry, smiling at the friendly encounter.

"Well, there she is," sang a thin gentlemen's familiar scratchy voice. He stood with others seeking reprieve from the sun in the shade of the porch roof.

"You're looking all shined up tonight, Herald." I noted the slacks, button-up shirt and a tie replacing the normal blue jeans and t-shirt. "What's the occasion?"

"Just for the comments," he laughed.

Several people waited on the bench attached to the building. "Hey, Nancey," one of them called to me. "What happened to the big guy who used to serve? I think it was just on Mondays."

"You mean Jim?" I moved closer to talk.

"Yea, he always had a smile and was so cheerful."

"He hasn't been here for a while because he went on a world tour. But I know he's back. I'll give him a call to tell him we miss him," I told her before going inside. I realized that I did miss him. His presence brought a feeling of compassion and love. I guess I wasn't the only one who enjoyed his comfort and encouragement.

The aroma of fish encircled me as I closed the door and crossed the busy kitchen to set my purse in a cupboard and place a sack of plastic containers next to the sink to be washed and used for take-out food. I washed my hands while greeting the other volunteers. Kandi was explaining to Webb, a new cook, what pan to place the fish in for serving. Annie was mixing the dressing into a large bowl of lettuce salad. Charlene was pouring juice into the plastic glasses.

I was still tying my apron when Kandi announced it was time for prayer. The small group of volunteers held hands and I offered a prayer for our guests as well as for each of us.

Genna unlocked the door and greeted each person as they stepped into the cool building. She stopped a petite girl in a loose fitting bikini top. "You don't have enough on. You can eat if you agree to wear this." Genna handed her a t-shirt from a stack nearby that was just for that reason.

The girl flipped strands of blond hair from her face. Her blue eyes glanced from Genna to the shirt. "Ok." She smiled and quickly slipped into the clean shirt.

In the kitchen, Webb served the catfish and baked potato. I added bread, and corn dipped in butter. Annie served lettuce salad and cucumber salad and offered tartar sauce, butter and sour cream. Betty served the dessert on a small paper plate.

"Do you have something besides fish?" asked one of the long-time patrons. We knew she was allergic to fish and prepared for her, and others that also may be allergic, a chicken and rice casserole. Webb went to the stove and scooped a serving on to her plate.

"No bread," someone requested as the line moved. "Can I have two butters and no sour cream?" someone else asked. "Smells good," another commented as he received his plate. The line flowed by for 25 minutes, followed by people returning for seconds.

"I just want fish and corn," said one man. Others wanted only fish and salad or cucumbers.

A thin blond came through and avoided our eyes as her lip trembled. Her face was stained with tears when she returned for seconds. In a shaking voice she told us how her dog had just been stolen. She reported the loss of her companion to the police. My heart ached as I thought of the recent death of my dog. "I'm so sorry," was all that I could offer.

"Hey, John, you look tired tonight," I said when a sandy-haired young man returned for more food.

He nodded. "I didn't get any sleep last night. Someone was outside. I'm guarding my things and my parent's tent, too, so I stayed awake to keep watch on things."

"I hope you get more sleep tonight," I said, handing him a plate of food.

Genna moved around the tables, picking up trays or used dishes and visiting with the guests. "You owe the money," a loud voice drew her attention to the back of the dining hall. She hurried to intervene.

"You need to quiet down," her pleas went unheard by the two arguing women as they stood across the table from one another. "You need to calm down." Genna put her arm between them as they began to lean forward. "You need to take this outside," she demanded between their searing words and threats. One went toward the door with two men. The second followed, accompanied by another man.

Genna and Kandi followed them to the parking lot where the women continued yelling at each other. One rode away on her bike, calling more insults as she left.

Outbursts in the dining hall were unusual. Arguments were generally defused by a volunteer's intervention before the situation escalated. Police were called only if the conflict threatened to become physical.

Recalling the angry voices, I noted the contrast with the friendly greeting I saw earlier. The mix of personalities was as varied here as anywhere in society. And each one should be treated fairly and with respect. When that gets hard, we need to remember what Jesus said in Matthew 25:40, "whatever you did for one of the least of these brothers of mine, you did for me."

Back inside, the many people around the dining hall continued as though nothing happened. Conversations continued, volunteers cleared tables and cleaned plates. The event was soon forgotten.

As the tables emptied, the volunteers started setting chairs on top of them to easily sweep and mop. When the entire dining hall was mopped, the chairs were returned to the floor and the tables were washed with bleach-water.

Left over fish, potatoes and dessert were placed in small containers, dated and left in the refrigerator to be given out later. The salad and cucumbers were set out in plastic containers for anyone to take home. There was no corn left over. Kandi took the bread, which can't be used again, home to her pigs.

In the kitchen, the crew moved mats, mopped floors and washed pans and dishes. The hallway was vacuumed and the restroom cleaned. By 6 p.m. the kitchen was once again clean and ready to greet the next group of diners.

Sample Menu:
Taco Casserole
Spanish Rice
Chips
Green Salad
Blueberries
Dessert

Dices the Attitude

People don't care how much you know, until they know how much you care.

Kevin Leman and William Pentak

Cynthia stood in the doorway with her broad shoulders squared and her jaw set firm as she handed the papers to an older woman. Cynthia's eyes stared at the paper as if her piercing glare could change the duration of her time in working at the Soup Kitchen or eliminate the sentence all together.

Joyce, who assisted the people sent to the Soup Kitchen by Community Services, read over the papers. Looking up at Cynthia, she recognized the hardened expression of resentment. "Ok, Cynthia, you can start by washing your hands and getting an apron on," she gently said as she walked into the kitchen. She stopped and waited for Cynthia, who still stood in the doorway as if some invisible barrier prevented her from following. "The sink we use for washing our hands is right here," Joyce gestured to her left. "The aprons are in the bottom drawer next to the sink."

Cynthia gave a heavy sigh as she took the few steps to the sink. She turned the faucet on and swung her hands through the cascading cold water. Joyce never raised her gaze from the paper she returned to reading, "Use hot water and soap, and be sure to use the brush around your fingernails." Cynthia grimaced but followed the instructions.

"This is Helen, one of the cooks," Joyce introduced an elderly lady carrying cans to the work counter.

"Hi," Helen's large smile wrinkled the edges of her green eyes.

147

Cynthia moved her head in acknowledgement but her lips remained tightly pursed.

Joyce accompanied Cynthia to the dining area. "This is Debbie. She'll be helping you," Joyce introduced a dark-haired girl in her twenties before returning to the kitchen.

"This you're first time?" Debbie asked as she sat a small bucket on the table in front on them.

Cynthia's lip curled into a sneer and her eyes narrowed, "Ya," she groaned.

"It's really kinda fun," Debbie laid some dishcloths next to the buckets and some on a little table behind them. "This is bleach water for wiping the trays as people bring them to you. Then dry them, place a napkin in the center and put them on the little table. When you get a bunch stacked, take them over there," she pointed to a stack of trays ready to use on a long table where the serving line started. "You can use the spatula to scrape off the plates into the can," She pointed to a large garbage can at the end of the table. "The liquids can go in this pitcher. Plates and glasses stack in these dishwasher trays and the silverware goes in this one." Debbie looked around the area, "Well, that's all there is to it."

Cynthia stepped back as the volunteers held hands in a circle for prayer. Outstretched hands encouraged her to join the group. Reluctantly, she held out her hands for the others to hold. She studied each person as they bowed their head. Their faces held a peace. Joyce's voice flowed with words of praise and thanksgiving, which were unfamiliar to Cynthia.

Following the prayer, the doors were opened and a line of hungry people filed in. Nervously, Cynthia shifted her feet while wringing the cloth in her hand. Her eyes were fixed on the trays as people handed them to her. Wipe, dry, place napkin and stack. She repeated her job until the last plate was taken to the kitchen.

She was glad it was busy and there had been no time for idle talk. Debbie showed her how to stack chairs on the tables, mop the floor, return the chairs to their place and wipe the tables with bleach water. When she put the mop away, her arms were too tired to hold their rigid stance. She removed her apron and hurried toward the door.

"Thanks for your help," Joyce called after her, unsure if she heard.

The next serving night, Cynthia was late. The prayer had already been said. *Sorry, I missed that,* she smiled to herself as she took her time washing her hands and getting an apron.

"You're behind." Debbie pointed to the stack of trays and dirty plates.

Cynthia picked up a rag and began to wipe a tray. "I'll help you," offered a boy who looked like he could be in his early teens. "I like to help when

I can." He began to dry and stack the trays. "I come here to eat with my mother," he pointed to a large lady at a nearby table. "It don't seem right to eat and not help out." He suddenly extended his hand toward her. "I'm Darren."

Cynthia's eyes narrowed as she looked at Darren and then his hand. She brushed a lock of her uncombed hair from her face and held her hand out for him to shake. She was thankful for Darren's help as more trays and plates kept adding to her work. Darren worked quickly, making Cynthia do the same. Darren talked as quickly as he worked. Cynthia occasionally nodded her head as if listening. As Darren left that night, he cheerfully talked with everyone he passed on his way to the door. *How can he be so happy when he has to eat here?* She wondered.

Joyce thanked Cynthia for her help each night. *She thanks me like I have a choice to be here,* Cynthia grumbled to herself.

Other volunteers cheerfully greeted her by name. Darren sometimes helped her after he had eaten and sometimes he visited with other guests, picking up their plates as they finished. Cynthia curiously watched from her position behind the clean-up table. Most of the people knew each other and the volunteers. Conversations flowed from all areas of the dining room. "Leah, that yellow shirt looks nice on you," someone complimented a dark haired woman. "How's that baby doing?" A volunteer asked, carrying a tray for a young mother with an infant in her arms.

Cynthia began arriving in time for the prayer and gripped the hands next to her. The idea of praying was new to her but she felt good to hear the soothing words.

If she came early, there was time to visit with Debbie before they were busy. Debbie talked about the classes she was taking at the community college and her part-time job and how much she enjoyed volunteering in the Soup Kitchen. Debbie seemed excited about everything and was always happy.

Most people were cheerful at the Soup Kitchen. She understood the volunteers being happy, but the guests were also friendly and caring towards each other. Some of the stories of their lives were sad. They had hard, difficult circumstances. She was embarrassed to think how she felt sorry for herself with her own situation.

"Thank you." Cynthia smiled as a small girl handed her a plate and glass.

Darren waved goodbye as he left for the night. "See you Wednesday," Cynthia waved back. "Don't forget the book you promised to let me read." Darren laughed and held his hand up with his thumb and index finger forming an 'O'.

Darren brought the book and they talked about chapters as Cynthia read. Debbie joined their discussions when time would allow. Others occasionally offered an opinion on the topic they were discussing. No one belittled her for anything she said. No one told her that her opinion was wrong. They listened to her and she listened to them, happy to learn what others thought.

Joyce met Cynthia while she was washing up one evening. "Cynthia, you only have two hours left of community service," she explained while looking over the papers Cynthia gave her the first evening. "After tonight, you are finished. I'll mail your time card to the office."

Cynthia dried her freshly cleaned hands and stood in the kitchen doorway. The edges of her mouth lowered, "I'm done?"

"Yes," Joyce confirmed the milestone that most community service workers looked forward to.

Cynthia looked up at her favorite cook placing the evening meal in the serving table. Two other volunteers poured juice and milk. "It's time to pray," called Faye, the manager, to the group of volunteers busy with the final preparations.

"Joyce," Cynthia softly spoke. "Do I have to leave after tonight?"

Joyce hesitated as she thought of Romans 12:21, "do not be overcome with evil, but overcome evil with good." She looked at Cynthia's silky auburn hair, curling neatly across her shoulder and the glimmer in her hazel eyes. Joyce saw the good that had overcome a hardened heart. "You are welcome to help as long as you want."

"I'll be back on Friday," Cynthia sang as she hurried to join the circle for prayer.

Sample Menu:
Sloppy Joes
Mixed Vegetables
Green Salad
Pears
Dessert

Toasts A Friend

Friendship isn't about whom you have known the longest;
but about who came and never left your side.

Author Unknown

The fierce bulldog emblem emerging from the front of his weathered cap did not reflect the kind person beneath. The rugged man, worn by years of hard living, most likely adopted the name, Bulldog, because of his scarred face and his dog-like 'woof, woof,' that he was fond of startling or greeting others. Unlike the growling, teeth-bared dog that sat atop his shaggy, dark hair threaded with silver, Bulldog was a caring spirit referring to those around him as 'sister' or 'brother.'

With his fist pounding the air above his head, he would bark out a deep "Woof, woof, woof." But then he would reach out with a sun-baked hand and say "All the respect." He respected others and expected it in return.

In line at the Lebanon Soup Kitchen, he smiled a greeting to the volunteers as he picked up a serving tray and placed it on the counter. "Thank you, sister, (or brother)" he acknowledged each server as they added a course to his meal. Friends greeted him as he carried his tray to a long table to join them.

He was a regular at the kitchen. His jovial bark and smile earned him many friends.

"He would always be welcomed at my table," Donnie reflected while eating the evening's warm meal. "He was fun to be around, if he wasn't too inebriated. I didn't like him sober, though," a wide smile erupted into a devilish grin.

Bulldog always had a story to tell and any observation could turn into a story, carried by his imagination. "One time he was telling a story of falling off a dock and was backing up while he talked until he fell off the end of the dock," Donnie laughed, remembering the man who could entertain most gatherings. "He was the life of the party. He had everyone laughing. If someone was down he'd put an arm around a shoulder and say 'don't be that way.' He lifted you, brought out the best.

"He always made a lasting impression. Sometimes good, sometimes not-so-good but mostly GREAT!" Donnie raised his voice and punched his hand above his head.

Across the table, Danimal smiled in agreement. "Bulldog gave me this name, a play on my real name. I sometimes play karaoke down by the river. Bulldog did the best he could. He might sing or just 'woof' into the mike. Bulldog loved music."

Smiling across the table Daisy talked freely and quickly when asked about Bulldog. "He was the first one I met when I came here (Soup Kitchen). It was at that back table." She pointed toward the end of the room lined with tables. "I asked him if he minded if I sat down. He said, 'You don't want to do that.' I asked him why and he said, 'Because you're a lady and ladies don't like a guy like me.' I just told him, if you can put up with it, I can too. We were friends after that."

Part of Daisy's neatly combed hair was pulled back and held in a band, leaving the rest to settle on her shoulders. Her blue eyes held a shine that accented her continual smile. "This was his social hour, his friends were here." Chewing a bite of food, she held a finger up signaling another thought. When she swallowed, she smiled as if telling a secret, "He loved children," nodding to assure it was true.

Daisy had two boys, ages nine and 12. They often came with her for meals. "My kids see it as a sense of safety at the Soup Kitchen. It's generally thought to be a rough crowd and you do have to be cautious." She picked a particle from her cavity-filled teeth. "Bulldog appreciated manners and he showed my boys that. I like what he has taught my kids. We need more Bulldogs in the World.

"He did meth for awhile but quit because it made him mean. It makes people mean and he didn't like mean people. But he never condemned anyone.

"One time I saw him down at the Starlite Tavern. He sat alone at a table to the side of the room with his bottles arranged in just the right spot in front of him. I waved for him to join me and my friends. He just waved back. Later, I asked him why he didn't join us. He said "It's best I party alone, don't get into trouble that way."

"I asked him one cold night if he was warm enough. He curled his lip into a toothless grin, "You don't have to worry about the old dog."

"Bulldog in the park was like having swings in the park, they just belonged. He got kicked out of the park for barking. There was this guy, who didn't look like a street person, who complained about Bulldog. He was just a mean person. One time he tried chasing Bulldog out of the park. Bulldog's not going to fight so he ran with this guy after him, barking the whole time. He got kicked out after that."

She shook her head with regret and continued, "Bulldog may have been through a lot and did some bad things, but he had a sense of innocence about him. He was a danger to no one. Some people said "you should have known him before he started drinking, he was so precious." Well, they should have known him after he drank. He was precious."

Teresa sat alone at the end of a table, her thick, dark hair tangled in the straps of the two backpacks she carried, even while seated. "I'm glad he died sober. He was a courageous, brave man, who survived through hard times," Teresa expressed between bites of her meal. "He liked to say 'hi' to me, asked how I was doing." She brushed the unkempt strands of hair falling over her brown eyes toward the edge of her face, just far enough to reveal the roundness of her checks.

"What Bulldog went through made me feel more fortunate for what I went through. I never got kicked out of a park. He had a harder time than I have." Teresa said, minimizing her own sad childhood and tough life.

She pushed the dark-rimmed glasses, weighted with thick lenses, up her nose, "I am glad they had a memorial dinner and glad I spoke at the service. It felt good to see so many speak at the service."

At another table across the busy room Vicky slid her nearly empty plate away. Her blue eyes sat like gems in her long, narrow face. Her short, straight hair hung loosely but was well kept. A Texas drawl gave evidence to her origins. "I met Bulldog at the Starlite bar down town, three years ago. I went to leave and he said, "Wait, Sister. You don't need to walk alone in the dark." After that, he would walk me home. If he saw me at the store, he would carry things home for me. He was a real sweet person. He started looking after me. His own situation never overshadowed his concern for others."

Sitting on the bench in front of the Soup Kitchen, moisture formed in Howard's reddened eyes as he thought about his friend, "He was one of the most honest people I have met. I would not be afraid to leave anything with him. He would say "in honor" and treated everyone with respect. He'd always start by saying "may I," like "may I ask you." He had good morals." Howard sucked in a deep draw from his rolled cigarette. "He'd drink. I'd drink. Sometimes it gets out of hand." The tears thickened as he looked away remembering some past conflict that was better left unspoken. I hoped that he could forgive himself, as well as Bulldog, for any unresolved conflict, like Colossians 3:13 teaches, "bear with each other and forgive whatever grievances you may have against one another. Forgive as the Lord forgave you."

Howard crushed his cigarette on the walk, tossing the butt in the sand tray. "He was never one to snivel and he'd help anyone. He had his checks maybe three days, that's how willing he was. Some took advantage of him because of it.

"He was chased around a lot, got kicked out of parks. There was this guy at the park who had a grudge against him, would go to all the parks and call the cops when he found Bulldog. He'd been 86ed from every park because of that "bounty hunter" harassing him." His dark eyes were dull as he stared at the cold cement between his feet. "Bulldog was living with Jimmy near the scrap-yard. He'd walk to the bridge and talk to us but wouldn't come into the park. He didn't want to go to jail." Howard continued, with a quiet, somber voice. "I think he spent more of his life in than out of jail."

Suzie fidgeted on the wooden bench next to Howard. Her eyelashes were lightly brushed with mascara above the soft slope of her cheeks. Her dark hair was pulled into a ponytail with a few strands resisting the bundle. The edges of her mouth rose to reveal one lone tooth while lifting her tanned checks closer to her attractive eyes framed with crow's-foot. "He always honored me," she added, her eyes lighting with pride.

Bulldog became a regular at the Soup Kitchen. One of the volunteers, Patty, grew to be a close friend. "Bulldog was leaving one evening and I slipped a sandwich in his pocket to take with him. He got a big grin and twinkle in his eye, "I know just who that could go to." He always gave to others."

One evening rhythms of a guitar, accompanied by a piano, flowed through the Soup Kitchen dining hall. Guests sang along with delight to gospel songs. Enthusiastically, Bulldog stomped his foot, waved his arms above his head and sang along with *I'll Fly Away*. The sparkle in his eyes did not reflect his alcohol level, but his joy of life.

Bulldog's prized possession was his two-inch by three-inch identification card with his picture on it, verifying that Darold Lee Williams existed.

Another possession that was important to him was his bicycle. Friends in Brownsville bought him one but it was soon stolen. Volunteers at the Soup Kitchen took a collection and replaced it. Again it disappeared, only to return and disappear again. The disappearing acts took place when he went into The Knot Hole store to purchase beer. His bike would be gone when he came out and materialized after Bulldog sobered up a little.

Rumors were someone felt it wasn't safe for Bulldog to be riding his bike while he was so inebriated.

Eventually, his bike was truly stolen which lead to his death. Bulldog missed his bike and was eager to get it back. While crossing the Grant Street Bridge, Bulldog saw a bike settled on the bottom of the Santiam River. He and his friend, Jimmy, began a project to retrieve it. At the water's edge, Bulldog tied a rope around his waist and gave the other end to Jimmy, who climbed the bank to the street and out onto the bridge. Holding the rope, Jimmy watched Bulldog's movements as he entered the water. While Bulldog paddled across the river, Jimmy dropped the rope. Maybe the rope was too short, or maybe it was a signal that Bulldog was above the submerged bike. The reason was unclear, leaving another mystery in his life story.

Weighted by the wet rope, Bulldog began to struggle toward shore. Jimmy ran from the bridge, over the embankment and to the water's edge to find Bulldog clinging to a rock in the river. Slowly, Bulldog motionlessly slid down the rock and disappeared into the deep waters, the rope acting as a weight to hold him under. A nearby construction worker helped Jimmy reach Bulldog and pull him to shore.

Rescue workers revived him with CPR at the river and then again in the ambulance. At the hospital, shock paddles restored a rhythm to his heart but could not return life to his body.

Life-support was disconnected but his breathing continued. The family paid their last respects and left to wait for the inevitable phone call.

Bulldog had many friends among the homeless and the Soup Kitchen. Ten of those came to the hospital for a last visit.

His friend Patty's heart ached when she heard the news. She was out of town and prayed that she could see her friend one last time. She arrived at his bedside on Monday. Her soft hands petted his rough checks as she told him how much she loved him, believing her voice transcended the barrier of the coma.

Bulldog's hair remained matted from the river water. Patty washed it and his silver beard and worked the beard into a long braid. In swabbing his dry lips, she discovered that he had two lower teeth that had not been visible in his smile. Her gentle voice read the newspaper articles of his accident to him. She talked to him. And she prayed.

"I told him to ask God what he should do; stay here if he could use his body again or to take the Lord's hand and keep walking." He went with the Lord at 4 a.m. Thursday.

Patty felt sad but relieved at the end. She was thankful that she now knew where he was and that he was not drunk. When he was alive, she worried.

She, along with his sister, Marge, felt bad that Bulldog was revived at the river only to have to die again.

Bulldog laid in a coma for six days. During that time, Patty told people about the homeless in Lebanon. A doctor and one of the nurses visited with Patty while checking on Bulldog. Both became interested in the Soup Kitchen and volunteered for a time. The young nurse thanked Patty for the care and compassion she showed.

When Patty heard that Bulldog was to be buried in his hospital gown because his only clothes had been cut off him and discarded at the hospital, she took clothes to the funeral home for him to be dressed with the dignity he deserved. Marge was told by the funeral home that there was no need to bring clothes. She was glad to find out that Patty had provided some.

Many people came to the services for Bulldog at the First Christian Church, the home of the Soup Kitchen. The table at the front of the sanctuary held his picture, surrounded by his meager possessions; his cap, with his namesake, and his tattered bandana joined his worn boots around his picture. Vases were set in the boots and wildflowers lay across the rear of the table. As people came forward to speak about their departed friend, each placed a flower in the vase-lined boots. At the end of the service the boots were full of colorful bouquets. The sanctuary filled with warmth and love for a man the world may never see as great, but others knew differently.

His cherished ID and wallet were buried with him. After the service his remaining possessions were given to several friends of his. His leather jacket, that he was never without, stayed in the homeless community to protect someone else from the cold. He would have been proud to share.

"The out-pouring of affection was eye-opening," said Patty. "The family was overwhelmed by the generosity of the church and the Soup Kitchen."

Between Marge, Patty and the Soup Kitchen, there was more than enough food to share with those at the service. Chicken, pasta and cake were taken to Bulldog's friends who preferred to remain in the park to toast their drinking buddy. The food taken to them also fed many others who had just arrived in the park after their homeless camp closed. In the end Bulldog continued to share with whoever needed help.

"Bulldog had a good sense of humor, friendly to everyone. He never said anything bad about anyone. He was a real likeable guy." Gentleness edged into the husky voice of one of the guests, "he was well loved by everyone here. He will be missed."

Sample Menu:
Beef Stew
Bread Sticks
Potato Salad
Banana Pudding
Dessert

Courtesy of Patty L.

Bulldog

A Savored Life

Choices are the hinges of destiny.

Pythagoras

At a booth in a small café, Bulldog's sister, Marge, sat with her husband, Tom. Her image reflected in the window as she spoke. "He didn't have to live on the street; he chose to," Marge's eyes moistened. "The rest of us (siblings) settled down and made a living. He wanted the lifestyle of the streets." She tried piecing together what she knew of Bulldog's often mysterious life.

Bulldog was born Darold Lee Williams. His twin brother, Jarold, died shortly after birth. A sister died in infancy and two brothers were killed as young adults, one in a car wreck and the other shot. Two siblings, Marge and Robert, lived in Sweet Home.

His father was a logger and the family moved several times in Bulldog's youth. While in Florence, Oregon, he had his first encounter with the law when a police officer caught him with a large knife and he was placed on probation. He then went to live with a family in Sutherlin where he participated in his 8th grade school programs. His family would travel to watch him sing in plays.

Bulldog's drinking problem began early when he and his brothers would pick blackberries or grapes to make wine, which he was fond of. Bulldog began high school in Sweet Home, not finishing the first year. He received a masonry diploma and a plumbing certificate but his drinking often cost him his job.

He started living like a hobo. Jumping railcars eventually took him to nearly every state in the country. "He was a wanderer who loved to travel," according to his close friend, Patty.

While traveling, he would seek out churches that provided food and sometimes traded work for shelter. Somewhere in The South, he lived with a minister and his wife and worked around the church. He called Marge from there and told her that he had found the Lord and stopped drinking. Months later he called and was drunk again. "He could have learned the Bible while there or maybe in prison." Marge took a sip of her coffee.

Around 1980, he was working for a wrecking yard in Independence, Oregon. While swimming on his day off, he dived into the water and broke his neck. Marge visited him in the Salem hospital during his recovery but when he was released it was years before she heard from him again.

Scars trailing across Bulldog's forehead, others rising above his mouth and his flattened nose were evidence of the harsh life that faced the homeless. The circumstances of the beating that nearly took his life were unclear, except that it took place in Kentucky.

The first time Bulldog went to prison was for drinking, driving without a license and breaking probation. The second time in prison, his brother, Joe, was also there. They began weight lifting. Bulldog set a record at Oregon State Penitentiary for most repetitions of the back-curl.

Another time in prison, Bulldog became friends with Joe, his nephew. One sunny afternoon, I sat with Joe on the deck of his mother's home. He lit a cigarette, throwing the match in a crowded ash tray. "I met him in the park before I knew he was my uncle. I was 19 or 20 when we met in prison."

Joe talked fondly of his uncle. "He had a lot of honor, was straight forward, friendly, polite and respectful. He was welcome wherever he went. When I was with him, I was welcome." He paused for drag from his cigarette. "He was really smart, was connected and had a sense about him, not everyone knew that. If he knew you, he'd openly talk. He didn't like being tied to one spot. He wasn't homeless. It was his lifestyle by choice.

"Bulldog told me he got his name in prison when some guys wouldn't let him and his friends use the weights. The other men stood their ground but he "bulldogged" his way through them."

The nickname and identifying bark were a mystery to his family. "My husband called one day and said he was bringing Bulldog home. I told him we didn't need any dog. That was the first time I had heard Darold called that," Marge laughed.

Bulldog often told partial stories, leaving out many details. One was that he had a son. He would not tell the son's name, age or whereabouts. He only said that when the child's mother, whether his wife or girlfriend was unclear, came to the Albany jail to pick him up after his release, she was hit by a car and killed. According to Bulldog, he then took the baby and hopped a train to Texas where he acquired a house and in later years gave it to the son.

In 2002, he was arrested in Reno for urinating on the street (which was a habit he never gave up). He requested time out of jail to go to Oregon to his mother's funeral. He was released, given a bus ticket and told never to return. The ticket took him as far as Medford. He never made it to his mother's funeral but eventually returned to Sweet Home.

His brother, Robert, provided a camper behind his house in Sweet Home for him to live in. Not long after Bulldog moved in, a foul odor began drifting from the camper. Robert investigated Bulldog's cluttered home and found packages of meat in various stages of rotting under the thin mattress. Bulldog had to leave.

Bulldog moved from one make-shift forest camp to another several times before living in a camp trailer behind his deceased brother's wife, Kay's home in Sweet Home. She sadly spoke about Bulldog from a swing on her deck, overlooking the camp trailer, "I was shocked how unkempt and dirty he looked. I hadn't seen him in years. He just showed up. I felt sorry for him, gave him a trailer to live in." She swung gently, staring across her backyard. "He would fight with himself when he drank. Literally, punching at himelf in the arms or stomach. The neighbors didn't like the noise he sometimes made in the middle of the night. He had to move."

Bulldog spent time in Sanky Park, where he would buy beer for teens in order to get a few beers for himself. Jeff, pastor of The Rev, a church in Foster, often brought his dog to the park and visited with Bulldog. "He tried to stay clean when he got out of jail, but alcohol was his biggest problem. Sometimes he was just not mentally there." Jeff's description confirmed the words of Proverbs 20:1, "wine is a mocker and beer a brawler; whoever is led astray by them is not wise."

Another member of the church, Jim, also befriended Bulldog and often invited him to church. Once Jim told Bulldog that he would pick him up for a special event at the church. The time came to pick him up and Jim tried to renege, "Bulldog smelled bad and was slobbering drunk, so I didn't want to take him. He tried to flag me down in my car but I didn't stop. A lady gave him a ride to the church though." Jim shook his head with a sigh. "Pastor Jeff dealt with him during the service. Whenever Bulldog started to holler, Jeff, who weighs 300 lbs, would pinch him in the side and twist flesh. Bulldog would sit down and be quiet.

"Following the service that night Bulldog cried and gave himself to God. He stayed afterwards for extra prayer," a smile eased across Jim's tanned face and lit his dark brown eyes.

For a time, Bulldog lived around Brownsville where he met Bruce. The church Bruce attended held a Thanksgiving dinner and Bruce invited Bulldog to join them. The church dining hall was decorated for the feast and filled with people dressed fittingly for the celebration. Bulldog entered the festive room with moss in his beard, leaves in his hair and mud on his clothes. The congregation watched in silent bewilderment as Bruce hurried to greet him and direct him to a seat next to his wife, Melinda, who hadn't been forewarned of Bulldog's possible arrival.

"I would lean toward any guy that walked by and take a deep breath just to avoid Bulldog's odor." Melinda's throaty laugh faded to seriousness. "But I tell you, he sat there with great pride. Some people reacted with disgust, some were reluctant, but in time many warmed to him."

Bruce's brown eyes narrowed as he talked of Bulldog. "I would see him at the store and buy him breakfast, because I knew he was always hungry. Bulldog scared people at first but when he had been around a while others began buying him meals. They learned not to give him money."

One time, cold rain soaked through Bulldog's entire wardrobe, which was on his back, his eyes were red and sniffles were woven through his sentences. An occasional cough interrupted his conversation with Melinda. Worried about his health, she called the police and made up a story to have him taken to jail, so he could get warm. The police wouldn't arrest him and Melinda was heartsick by the words of one of the officers, "The last time I took him in it took three weeks to get the smell out of my car. I wish he'd just die so none of us had to deal with him anymore." Melinda sadly shook her head, "He got his wish."

Marge helped Bulldog when she could and sometimes gave him a ride to town when he moved to a brushy area near Lebanon. The site had a couch and chair arranged around a fire pit. Once, when Marge and Bulldog returned to his camp, his belongings were gone. With a shake of his head all he said was, "Those good buddies of mine."

Marge invited Bulldog to family gatherings. Occasionally, he joined them. One Thanksgiving he arrived with soiled clothes and an offensive odor that covered the aroma of the cooking turkey. Marge suggested he use the shower while she found him clean cloths. "No," he explained, "I've been in the river and am fine."

Once a month, Bulldog would ride his bike on a loop from Lebanon through Brownsville to see friends, Crawfordsville to visit relatives and Sweet Home to pick up his Social Security check at Marge's home. "One time he had a flat tire and called to borrow money to fix it." Marge took a drink from her coffee. "When his next check came, he asked me to take him to the bank to cash it and paid me back. He was good about paying me back."

Marge returned home from a camping trip to feed the cat and water plants. Her plans to rejoin her family changed as a deputy told her to get to the Lebanon hospital immediately. She did not know why.

She learned at the hospital that Bulldog had been under water for 12 minutes and was revived three times. A CT scan showed that he was brain-dead and the doctor thought Bulldog died from a heart attack rather than drowning. The doctor suggested disconnecting the life-support system but Marge chose to wait for her family to be with her.

"I told Darold he was going to a better place and to just let go," Marge said, feeling lucky to have the chance to say goodbye. "I'll see him again if I'm lucky enough to go the same direction." Wiping moisture from her eyes, Marge continued. "At least we know where he is. If this had happened somewhere else, we may never have found out."

He is finally at rest with his family; buried in the large family plot at the Bellinger Cemetery.

Sample Menu:
French Toast Casserole
Pasta Salad
Watermelon
Dessert

Settles In

*The grand essentials to happiness in this life are something
to do, something to love and something to hope for.*

Joseph Addison

The Lebanon Soup Kitchen is a life-ring for many people, giving
them something to do, even if only an hour, 3 days a week. They
feel love and find hope for their own lives. The encouragement in the
compassionate volunteers is often the only light they see.

When the Soup Kitchen opened in 1989, Lebanon's population was
10,800. Today it is more than 13,000. The first year nearly 15,000 meals
were served at a cost of 56 cents a meal. The number of meals served peaked
in 2003 with 25,740 at a cost of $1.21 a meal. The first quarter of 2008 over
7,000 meals were served, costing $1.59 each.

The number of meals served is not the same as the number of people
who come for a meal. The count represents adults, kids, seconds or thirds
and take-home food given out. Take-homes may be premade sandwiches and
salads donated by local stores or leftovers from a previous night that are put
in small butter or yogurt containers. The seconds and take-homes can be
25% to 50% of the total count. The number of people served each night
varies from as low as 35 at the beginning of the month to 125 at the end of
the month.

The annual cost for food has risen from $8,544 in 1990 to $30,257 in
2007. Yet, even with rising expenses, the needs of the Soup Kitchen are always
met. "Whenever we need anything, it just falls out of the sky," is a common
explanation of Manager Janet Contreras. To keep His work operating, God
showers the Soup Kitchen with generous donations from individuals and
businesses.

Over the years the community recognized the work of the Soup Kitchen with many acknowledgements in awards, articles and appreciation letters. The latest one received was a Certificate of Appreciation from U.S. Department of Labor on May 1, 2008. It read in part, "...for your selfless and dedicated service as a Title V Host Agency for Experience Works. Thank you for making such a positive difference in the lives of Linn County's Older Workers." Experience Works helps older workers gain experience in order to qualify for jobs. Three people have been placed with the Soup Kitchen.

The Soup Kitchen began as a work for God and that dedication is reaffirmed by the volunteers forming a prayer circle before each meal. They pray for the people who come, as well as the people who serve. This openness to God allows His presence to be seen in even the smallest details. This book gives only a glimpse into the many ways He works. Volumes would be needed to record each story, because every person has a story.

The prophet Isaiah explains why God showers His blessings on the Soup Kitchen and its work, "Then you will call, and the Lord will answer; you will cry for help, and he will say: Here am I. If you do away with the yoke of oppression, with the pointing finger and malicious talk, and if you spend yourselves in behalf of the hungry and satisfy the needs of the oppressed, then your light will rise in the darkness, and your night will become like the noonday. The Lord will guide you always." (Isaiah 58:9-11a)

God brings people and situations together in miracles that bring blessings to those involved. One definition of a miracle is: an event or action that apparently contradicts known scientific laws. Someone may claim there are no miracles here, only coincidence. But also listed as a definition of miracle is: a remarkable thing. Many remarkable things happen every day within the Soup Kitchen. Learning to see those miracles takes awareness and gratitude of the One who created them. I hope that by reading these accounts you may see the miracles in your own life more clearly. Seeing and acknowledging God's work leads to gratitude, and gratitude creates hope.

The essentials of happiness are found by developing your awareness of God and His work. Love and hope are found in doing something, especially if it is for someone else.

If you have a story that you would like to share about yourself or someone you know who has contributed to the Soup Kitchen, you may sent it to me at the address below. I would be pleased to read it and possibly use it in further publications.

If you would like to help or would like more information, letters and donations may be mailed to:

Lebanon Soup Kitchen
170 E. Grant St.
Lebanon, OR 97355

Printed in the United States
129847LV00003B/166-498/P